Haunted Maine

Ghosts and Strange Phenomena
of the Pine Tree State

Charles A. Stansfield Jr.

Illustrations by Heather Adel Wiggins

STACKPOLE
BOOKS

In Honor of Walt and Eileen,
Eleanor, Chet, Herb, and George
And in Memory of Joan,
BeeJay, and Wade

Copyright © 2007 by Stackpole Books

Published by

STACKPOLE BOOKS
5067 Ritter Road
Mechanicsburg, PA 17055
www.stackpolebooks.com

Printed in the United States of America

10 9 8 7 6 5 4 3 2 1

FIRST EDITION

Library of Congress Cataloging-in-Publication Data

Stansfield, Charles A.
    Haunted Maine : ghosts and strange phenomena of the Pine Tree State /
Charles A. Stansfield, Jr.
        p.   cm.
    Includes bibliographical references.
    ISBN-13: 978-0-8117-3373-1 (pbk.)
    ISBN-10: 0-8117-3373-4 (pbk.)
    1. Ghosts-Maine. 2. Monsters-Maine. 3. Parapsychology-Maine 4.
Haunted places-Maine. I. Title.
BF1472.U6S726   2007
133.109741-dc22
                                                                    2006018546

Contents

Contents

Introduction

THERE IS A STORY THAT A FRIEND ASKED OF A WISE MAN, "DO YOU believe in ghosts?" "No," was his reply, "but I am afraid of them." Does that summarize your attitude as well? Then welcome to the club—very large club in membership, for most of us fall in the great "in-between" category when considering the supernatural. On one side are the true believers, who have no doubts whatsoever about the existence of ghosts. On the other hand are those who would express their disbelief strongly and repeatedly, equally certain in their skepticism. But for most of us we're not quite sure, are we?

There is one fact that commands complete agreement: Every human culture across the globe has traditions of ghosts, witches, demons, and haunted places. Race, ethnicity, language, religion, and history—all of these may vary, but long traditions and tales of hauntings, devils, monsters, and spirits, both good and evil, are present everywhere and among all peoples. Why are such stories universal? Why, for example, do the Navaho of America's southwestern desert still tell stories of how Navaho witches can "shapeshift," changing from human to animal form, becoming wolves or owls—an eerily similar tradition to central European tales of vampires who can turn into wolves or bats? Is it pure coincidence that these people so distant from one another and so very different in race, language, and religious tradition both have handed down similar stories across the generations?

Whether we are true believers or not, tales of the supernatural interest and entertain us. Through the lens of the ghost story, we can look at the world a little differently, and perhaps learn a little bit about ourselves, our beliefs, our fears, and even our cultural heritage. Whether we classify ghost stories and other tales of the unexplained as fiction or nonfiction, these stories help us to ponder the great mysteries of the nature of life and death.

Regional ghost stories like the ones found in this collection even have something to tell us about local history, culture, and geography. And they're fun—so enjoy! Maybe, just maybe, you'll even believe what you once doubted, but at least you'll appreciate some interesting stories.

This book begins with some general observations of the supernatural in Maine and then organizes stories by region. The coastal area of Maine, including most of Maine's people (and ghosts) is divided into four regions: The South Coast, from the New Hampshire border to Old Orchard Beach; the Greater Portland area; the Central Coast from South Harpswell to Bar Harbor; and Down East, the north coast from Winter Harbor to the Canadian border. The North Woods, inland from Tidewater, is the fifth region.

Maine Sailors' Superstitions

Sailors are a superstitious lot. After all, the sea is unforgiving and cruel. The ocean is a dangerous place to make a living, and many a sailor or fisherman has never returned from that last voyage. Maine sailors and fishermen especially share many deep superstitions, as the coast of Maine, fringed by a labyrinth of jagged islands and submerged rocks, often veiled in fog and beset by howling storms, is unusually dangerous.

Most who venture out to sea share a strong belief in "Jonahs." A Jonah is an unlucky, but not necessarily evil person. A Jonah aboard a ship will bring bad luck: If a Jonah sails on a fishing vessel, very few fish will be caught; if a Jonah is aboard a cargo ship, cargo will fall overboard. There have been many instances of a ship being "hoodooed" or cursed by a Jonah, only to regain its good luck when the Jonah left. Once a man is known to be a Jonah, he should change careers and stay ashore. If he persists in going to sea, eventually the ship that carries him will sink without a trace.

Seasoned sailors know to board a ship with the right foot the first to touch the deck. A ship should be boarded on its right, or starboard, side if at all possible.

Introduction

As the ship leaves the dock, someone should toss a penny into the water. This is tribute to Neptune, the ancient god of the sea. If Neptune doesn't get his tribute, he may see to it that the ship never returns. If you watch a ship out of sight, you will never see it again.

Some days are more favorable on which to begin a voyage than others. An old sailor's rhyme goes: "Sunday sail, never fail, Friday sail, ill luck and gale."

A horseshoe nailed to the mast protects against witches.

A cat aboard brings good luck, unless it falls overboard, which is an ill omen. Two cats aboard is bad luck. It is unlucky to bring an umbrella aboard a ship. It is unlucky to drive a nail on Sunday.

The name of the Lord must never, ever, be taken in vain aboard a ship.

If becalmed, the captain can "whistle up" a breeze by whistling a hymn. If you would have a fair wind at your back, stick a knife into a stern (back) side of a mast.

When fishing, toss back the first fish caught. That fish will lead others toward your boat. But the first fish caught on a fishing boat's first voyage should be nailed to the mast to ensure further luck in catching fish.

A silver coin should be placed under the base of a mast when the ship is under construction—this will keep the mast from falling in a storm.

A ship's name should not be made public until the launch. It is considered bad luck to change the name of a ship. To name a ship after a previous ship of the same type could be bad luck, or good luck, depending on the fate of that earlier ship. For example, it is said that many Maine residents begged the U.S. Navy to *not* use the name *Maine* on any new battleship after the *Maine* blew up in Havana Harbor in 1899, contributing to the start of the Spanish-American War. If that earlier *Maine* had been lost in battle, it would have been good luck to reuse the name, but *Maine* never fired her guns at an enemy before her destruction, and so hers was not a lucky name to pass on.

Bringing a caged bird aboard a ship could doom that ship. However, if a land-based bird like a sparrow or robin lands on a ship at sea, it is to be treated as an honored guest. Large, predatory birds like hawks, owls, or crows, bring bad luck if they land on a ship's rigging.

If a cake of ice accidentally falls overboard as a fishing boat is preparing for a voyage, that is very good luck. It is very bad luck, however, if a hatch cover is, when opened, allowed to fall on deck upside down.

If a sailor, on his way to board his vessel, meets a clergyman or a pregnant woman or a disfigured person, he should turn back home and not sail until the following day.

An albatross contains the spirit of a drowned sailor. It is bad luck if an albatross lands on a ship, but the bird must never be harmed or threatened.

Finally, if a porpoise accompanies a ship, entering or leaving harbor, this is good luck. A shark following in the wake of a ship is an evil omen. Two sharks practically guarantee disaster.

Childhood Witchcraft

Witchcraft was a major concern in early colonial Maine. Everybody talked about it. At its extreme, this fascination with witches and the supernatural degenerated into, quite literally, witch hunts. Many people, most likely innocent of any evil acts, were tortured and killed as witches. But many people—including curious, playful children—dabbled in divination, a practice to foretell the future. Just as in many popular parlor games of later centuries, colonial adults, teenagers, and even children entertained themselves with attempts at peering into the future. The infamous Salem Witch Trials of the late seventeenth century, for example, were the result of hysteria that began with a few young girls trying playfully to guess what their future husbands would look like.

A popular children's game in early Maine was to cut open an apple and count the seeds. The number of seeds found within would provide information about the apple-cutter's future love life and, ominously, a prediction that could be quite enlightening. The rules, in the form of a rhyme, are:

One (apple seed), I will love,
Two, I do love,
Three, my love is deep,
Four, I love with all my heart,

Five, I cast away,
Six, he loves,
Seven, she loves,
Eight, they both love,
Nine, he comes,
Ten, he tarries,
Eleven, he courts,
Twelve, he marries,
Thirteen, Satan find thee,
Fourteen, all the rest are little witches.

Of course, no one wanted to reach the count of thirteen. It was most unlikely anyhow—did you ever find that many seeds in one apple? The usual trick, if the seed count was getting close to a dozen, was for the child dissecting the apple to quickly pop a seed or two in their mouth. But this could be tricky. Apple seeds, it was believed, must be carefully chewed before swallowing. Swallowing an apple seed whole during the divination ceremony would cause the seed to sprout within the person, and tiny green leaves would appear in the person's navel. At that point, according to the logic of eight and ten year olds, the victim must be careful to cover the leaf buds with clothing and not allow them to received direct sunlight. In full sunlight, the apple tree would grow to great size in an instant, impaling its unlucky host on its trunk.

Now you know what to do in an apple-seed divination. Maybe you really shouldn't count the seeds.

Do Seagulls Contain the Spirits of Dead Fishermen?

There was a belief that seagulls must never be harmed in any way, for they carried within them the spirits of dead fishermen. This belief finds its roots in the dangerous Maine waters—notorious for sudden storms, frequent fogs, and a maze of rocky islands and submerged reefs and ledges. Many a fisherman has failed to return to port safely, and those that do thank the seagulls for their safe landfall.

Gulls do not sing sweetly. In an all-avian competition, seagulls would not win any prizes for their raucous voices, which sound more like hoarse screams than anything else. It is those distinctive, loud cries, though, that are so valued by Maine fisher folk.

It is firmly believed by Maine coastal fisherman that seagulls can see further through fog than humans. Gulls, it is claimed, will scream warnings to fogbound boats coming too close to the cliffs in foggy weather, saving the fishing boats from being smashed on the rocks.

Also, gulls help fishermen find the fish; a school of fish near the surface will be spotted by gulls, which then repeatedly dive on them, screaming the reports of their find to other gulls and also to fishermen. And so the gulls are the fishermen's friends, warning of danger and reporting the whereabouts of fish. Gulls also are known to attend the funerals of fishermen, roosting in cemetery trees, respectfully silent as graves are filled in. Do the birds host the spirits of the dead? Maine fishermen aren't sure that they do, nor are they sure that they don't. But why take a chance? And why bother such a helpful bird, whether its warning cries of danger and its fish-discovery caws are intentioned as friendly gestures to people or are just gulls being gulls?

The "Luck" of the House

It is an old English tradition, or maybe an old English superstition, brought to Maine by early settlers that an object called a "luck" is the physical manifestation of the good fortune of the house and the family residing there. This family talisman is frequently a rather fragile object. Should this luck (never called lucky but always used as a noun) be smashed or stolen, evil will befall the family who lives there.

Colonial-era houses in Maine that are still occupied by descendents of their original builders most likely have such a luck. The owners will guard it carefully against damage or theft, for its powers to preserve the household against disasters depend on its unmarred physical presence in that house. Traditionally, the best lucks are those either given to the family as a gift or commissioned by the family to commemorate a noble or courageous act by a family member.

The tradition of the household luck traces back in England to the fifteenth and sixteenth centuries. Two famous lucks from that time were those of the Musgrave family at Eden Hall, Cumberland, England, and the Pennington family at Muncaster Castle.

Legend has it that the luck of Eden Hall is a Venetian glass goblet, thought to have been designed as a communion chalice. A beautiful example of enameled and engraved glass, it was a gift to the Musgraves from Mary, Queen of Scots. She gave it to the family in gratitude for their help when she was fleeing south from Scotland, having just been defeated in battle at Langside in 1568. The luck of Eden Hall is said to have had several narrow escapes but remains intact to this day, an inspiration to those "first families" of Maine who cherish their own legendary lucks.

The less happy history of the Pennington family luck at Muncaster Castle illustrates the evil consequences of inadequate protection. The Muncaster luck was a bowl of purple glass presented to the family by King Henry the Sixth to commemorate the occasion of their granting the King refuge following a disastrous battle at Hexham in the year 1463. Supposedly, the King's gift was enscribed, "As long as this bowl is unbroken, the Pennington family shall greatly thrive and never lack a male heir." And so the Penningtons of Muncaster Castle did thrive until 1917 when the last male heir was killed on a World War I battlefield in France. The bowl had been smashed accidentally the year before.

So if you, by chance, should happen to admire a fragile antique connected by legend to an old family's early history, be very careful. You may be, literally, holding the family's luck in your hands.

Indian Sacrifice Rocks

It is an ancient custom in many different lands for people to make offerings to their gods or powerful spirits. These gifts are intended to acknowledge the power of the god or spirit and earn its favor. In some religious traditions, these offerings are made to evil spirits in an attempt to turn aside their evil powers.

Early European accounts of Indian religious practices, which may have been biased against non-Christians, reported that the Indians of Maine made various offerings to an evil spirit, Hobomock, who would then refrain from working any evil spells upon those who sought to propitiate him.

The great French explorer, Samuel de Champlain, sailed along Maine's coast and wrote about the local Indians. When Indian guides helped Champlain navigate the lower reaches of the Sasanda River—which is one of the mouths of the Kennebec River near the present town of Bath—he noted that they placed arrows at the base of a promontory called Hobomock Head. The beautifully crafted arrows, which took much time and skill to make, were considered suitable gifts to Hobomock, who then would not interfere with the safe navigation of the twisted tricky channels of the Sasanda.

In the same tradition of placing gifts to Hobomock near or on potential hazards to safe passage, Champlain and others noted the local Indian custom of crowning dangerous rocks near shore with wreaths made of pine or oak boughs, or both. These were known as sacrifice rocks.

It is said that in the European colonial era and even long after, Maine sailors and fishermen would continue the Indian custom in their own way by tossing small coins at these sacrifice rocks as they passed by. You just can't be too careful along the rocky coasts of Maine.

South Coast

THE SOUTH COAST REGION STRETCHES FROM THE NEW HAMPSHIRE border at Kittery Point to Old Orchard Beach. While the South Coast is a relatively small region, its natural beauty attracts many visitors. This is the part of Maine that is most accessible to the residents of the great cities to the south.

The Witch's Chowder Recipe

People wonder why true New Englanders would never be caught dead eating Manhattan clam chowder. According to an obscure Maine legend, it is because they don't want to be *found* dead. There is a curse on so-called Manhattan clam chowder, and it was put there by a Maine witch.

This witch, the story goes, lived in Kennebunkport many years ago. Like most witches, Edith Tibbett was both a renowned cook and a staunch defender of old-time traditions.

Maine, like the rest of coastal New England, is blessed with an abundance of clams. In colonial times, it was customary for every family to own a clam rake and go out on the nearest tidal flats at low tide to dig up the makings of a good chowder. Every man, woman, and child knew how to make clam chowder, and they all loved to eat it too. Even the devil himself, it was claimed, enjoyed a bowl of chowder on occasion, so much so that he would forego his evil tricks for a few hours while he savored a bowl.

Auntie Edith, as she was known, was a good witch—one that used her powers more to help than to harass. She was especially famous for her clam chowder. This chowder, it was said, could make Satan himself smile. And sure enough, Satan did smile in contentment when he dropped by Auntie Edith's house for dinner, which he did on autumn nights with a full moon.

The devil is, by preference, a city boy, as cities are fertile ground for evil, so it is not surprising that he gets a bit nervous in the fresh air and clean living of the countryside. It is also not surprising that city life had given him a taste for Manhattan clam chowder. As all true New Englanders know, it is sacrilege to immerse the bivalves in the tomato-based, thin vegetable soup that Manhattanites mistakenly think is a chowder. The watery, acidic brew is an affront to all right-thinking New Englanders, especially to those who reside in Maine.

Thinking to degrade New England cuisine and thus demoralize the population, the devil suggested that Auntie Edith help popularize the Manhattan technique for drowning innocent clams. The good witch immediately understood the devil's motive. The sharper flavor of tomatoes would mask the off-taste of clams too long absent from saltwater, making food poisoning a more likely threat. No doubt, the devil would be entertained by the sight of people bent double in agony after eating bad clams. The milder taste of a true New England chowder wouldn't disguise the taste or aroma of a bad clam.

And so, in an effort to thwart the devil's evil plans, Auntie Edith let it be known that she had placed a curse on Manhattan clam chowder. Those who defied tradition and defiled their tables with the foreign swill would find their hair falling out, their stomachs upset, and their sex life nonexistent. Death would soon follow.

To avoid this curse, abstain from that obnoxious Manhattan culinary offense and use Auntie Edith's own recipe:

1 quart of clams, shucked that day
1/4 pound of salt pork, diced
6 large potatoes (Maine potatoes, of course)
2 large onions, diced
1/4 pound of butter

1 quart of milk
1 quart of cream
1 clove of garlic, whole, speared with a toothpick so it can be
    removed after cooking

Serve with freshly crumbled crackers floating on top. Do not serve to the Devil—if you do, he'll keep coming back for more.

How to Deal with the Devil

There are many stories about clever people outwitting Satan. Down near Kittery, people used to tell how Sarah Woodman dealt with the devil, or at least someone who claimed to be the devil. This happened long ago, but the lesson that Sarah demonstrated remains true today.

Sarah was a member of the Abnaki tribe, and she was a convert to Christianity. As a Christian, she knew about the devil, the personification of evil. She often wondered, as did many of her neighbors, if the real devil resembled the person of Nicholas Whitney, the local grouch. Nicholas looked like *a* devil, if not *the* devil. He was incredibly ugly, and his behavior was pure ugliness too. He was mean for the sake of being mean. He owned a great deal of land but was so lazy that little of it was ever plowed or grazed, and it began to revert to brush and wild trees.

That kind of half-forested abandoned farmland, as every hunter knows, attracts game animals and birds because it offers plenty of wild food. Huckleberries, wild grapes, butternuts, chestnuts, and walnuts were there for the taking. Not that Nicholas ever bothered to gather up the nuts and fruits, or hunt deer, rabbit, squirrel, or wild turkeys on his land. No sir, he was too lazy to do that.

But he was even meaner than he was lazy. He'd rather see the huckleberries rot on the bush than the neighborhood boys gathering them.

Sarah, having been reared in Abnaki ways, regarded nature's bounty as part of God's gift to his people. She never would take another person's food unless, of course, that other person neglected to gather up his share of nature's gifts. And so, Sarah regarded Nicholas's untapped food supply as hers to use, as she was not taking any food from her neighbor's mouth.

Nicholas just got madder and madder at Sarah's unauthorized visits to his land, so he decided to teach Sarah a lesson. When one of his bulls was butchered, Nick took the bloody hide, horns and all, and covered himself in it. Accompanied by some drunken buddies, he stomped over to Sarah's little house one evening at twilight to put the fear of the devil in her.

Sarah was hard at work in her garden, weeding by moonlight, industrious as ever. Nicholas, wrapped in the hide and wearing the bull's horns on his head, crowed like a demented monster. Sarah just kept on working. Nicholas continued to prance and roar. Sarah continued to ignore him.

"Woman, do you know who I am?" demanded the weird-looking creature. "No," was her reply as she calmly kept on doing her chores. "Well, I'm the devil!" he screamed. "Really?" she said, "then I feel sorry for you." At that point, Nicholas's drunken cronies saw the humor in all this, and burst out laughing at the "devil" who was unable to scare a solitary woman. Nicholas and his chums skulked back to their favorite tavern, where the would-be devil's fruitless visit became the subject of much scornful merriment. The imitation devil was made to look foolish indeed.

The whole neighborhood learned a lesson worth repeating over the generations: There's just one way to fight the devil. Just keep straight on with what you're doing and don't mind him, and he can't do anything to you.

And, by the way, do you think that Nicholas Whitney really could have been *the* "Old Nick" in disguise?

The Captain's Peg Leg

Down near Old Orchard Beach some oldtimers can still remember the legend of the captain's peg leg. It seems that in the early nineteenth century, a sea captain by the name of Edward Blackstone suffered a great misfortune: A shark bit off his leg. Now many sailors in the old days believed in a dark superstition that once a shark has tasted a bit of you, it will be back someday to finish its feast. That is, of course, if the victim doesn't first kill the shark in revenge. A man who has lost a chunk of himself to a shark is considered to be under a curse until that same shark is killed.

Following his brutal encounter, Captain Blackstone became possessed by two great compulsions. The first, of course, was to find and kill the shark that had snacked on his leg. The second was the care of his artificial leg, which, in those more primitive days, was a simple wooden spool much like the leg of a piece of furniture.

The captain had his peg leg crafted of the finest walnut. He personally waxed and polished it every day so that the wood gleamed. Cleaning and polishing that wooden appendage became almost an unhealthy fetish.

As for his other mission in life—the destruction of sharks, the captain soon earned a reputation as a fearless, and ruthless, shark hunter. He killed hundreds of sharks during his fishing trips to deep waters.

Many was the day, in fair weather or foul, when Edward Blackstone would strap on his peg leg and head out to sea. "There's sharks out there, I can smell them!" he'd declare. Then, finally, he insisted on venturing out during a howling winter gale. No one would go with him, so he sailed alone into the teeth of the storm. He never came back, at least not all of him—his peg leg washed up on the beach a few days later. It was returned to his widow, who placed it by the fireplace in her sitting room.

Strange things began to happen. Blackstone's widow began to hear strange tapping noises after she'd retired for the night. In the morning, the wooden leg would be in a different place than the preceding evening. Was the captain's peg leg going out on nightly shark hunts? This went on for weeks. Finally, one morning after a particularly stormy night, the widow Blackstone found her late husband's wooden leg on the floor by the fireplace, soaking wet. She called in the servant girl to chastise her, thinking that the girl had left open a window and let in the rain. "How else could the peg leg have gotten wet?" she asked. "I didn't leave any windows open, my lady," replied the girl, "and besides, taste that water in the puddle by the leg. It's saltwater!"

Now convinced that the peg leg was possessed, the widow sought advice from her clergyman. "Give the wooden leg a Christian burial" was his advice, which she followed. Once that was done, there were no more mysterious tappings at night, nor any more salty puddles on the floor. Perhaps the peg leg's final voyage on saltwater had produced another dead shark—the right one, finally.

The Legend of the Loups-Garous

Many French Canadians tell stories about the Loups-Garous, bewitched souls who must serve the devil for terms corresponding to their neglect of their Christian duties. Maine is blessed with many citizens of French Canadian heritage, so tales of Loups-Garous are common in the Pine Tree State. One of the most horrific accounts is about Pierre Dumont, who lived long ago on a farm near Ogunquit.

His neighbors couldn't figure out why Pierre was so prosperous. No one could recall ever having seen him work. The crops grown on his land always were of the finest quality and produced in unheard-of abundance. His lobster pots were always filled, and the fishing boat he owned always caught as big a haul as it could hold. His barns, fences, house, and sheds were kept in fine condition, always in good repair and freshly painted. In winter the trap lines in his woods always caught animals with the thickest, glossiest pelts. Prosperity seemed to live in his house, yet he seldom lifted a finger.

Dumont's neighbors heard weird noises at night coming from his property, so much so that they stayed well clear of his land. Whenever it was necessary to use the road that ran by his house, passersby would cross themselves and hurry on. It was rumored that Dumont was in league with the devil, and that would explain his effortless prosperity. Needless to say, Pierre Dumont never had visitors and never feared trespassers.

But late one night, a villager who had consumed way too much brandy decided to take a shortcut across Dumont's fields. As the foolish trespasser crossed Dumont's property, he heard a horrible noise. As he looked up, he witnessed an incredible sight: Sailing forty feet in the air was a huge, black rowboat, propelled by twenty oarsmen. The boat landed at Dumont's house and twenty bedeviled Loups-Garous lept out, chained together and cowering under a whip wielded by a tall man dressed entirely in red. The Loups-Garous went to work about the farm, doing all the chores that a successful farm required. "Harder, faster!" screamed their demonic master, "there is much work to be done!" It was clear that Pierre Dumont had sold his soul to the devil in return for the work of enslaved Loups-Garous.

The accidental witness to this devilish visit hurried to consult the parish priest. It was decided that they, along with half a dozen staunch churchgoers, would lay in wait for the devil that next night. The priest and the good men of his church arrived at Dumont's farm at nightfall. The priest sprinkled holy water over the land and then they awaited the midnight arrival of the devil's boat and its bewitched crew.

With the clamor of a freight train, the boat sailed overhead and glided down to Dumont's front yard. As the devil stepped out of the boat, however, he screamed in agony, as the holy water's touch burned him like hellfire. Groaning in pain, the devil jumped back into his magical boat, leaving the Loups-Garous behind. The men of the parish leaped forward, making small cuts on the arms of the Loups-Garous—causing the bloodletting that freed them from servitude to the Prince of Darkness. Pierre Dumont was struck by a bolt of fire flung down by the devil as he departed, and his soul was snatched up into the flying rowboat.

It is said that attendance at mass was improved greatly after that, and most villagers went to confession weekly. You must be sure not to become a Loups-Garous.

How the Witch Rode the Skipper

Down in Kittery, there was a crusty old fishing boat captain who was notoriously tightfisted with money. Most fishermen are careful with money, as their hard work seldom pays very well, but old Skipper Perkins was just plain mean. He wouldn't give away last week's fish scales if he could help it. He was never known to have a charitable impulse in his entire miserable life. Until, that is, a witch named Betty Booker taught him a lesson.

Life had not been kind or generous to old Betty Booker. Her husband, a fisherman, had been lost at sea. Many was the night that Betty went to bed without supper. Now Betty Booker had learned a thing or two about witchcraft, but she was too good a churchgoing woman to use the dark arts for personal gain; until she encountered Skipper Perkins, that is.

One fine day Betty came upon Skipper Perkins about to board his boat for a day's fishing. "Bring me back a nice cod, will you skipper?" she begged. "Show me your money," replied Perkins. "You know I have none," said Betty. "Then you'll see no cod," was the prompt reply.

Once out on the water, the weather turned nasty. The sea beat up his boat, and his nets caught nothing. As they say along the Maine coast, his boat came back poorer than it went. It was not a good day for Skipper Perkins, and it got worse. The rumor reached him that Betty Booker had made a witch's bridle—braided horse-hair stolen from a horse's tail on a moonless night—and was coming for him.

Perkins ran home and barricaded his doors and windows, but to no avail. A strong wind blew open his front door and there stood Betty with her witch's bridle. As though possessed of superhuman strength, Betty threw the bridle around the terrified skipper, made him get down on all fours, and rode him bareback down to the docks. She threw him off the dock into the cold water and commanded him, "Get me a nice cod, and make it a present!" Skipper Perkins somehow caught a cod with his own hands and gave it to Betty.

"Never refuse a fish to a penniless person again!" she said. And he never did from that day forward.

The Legend of Old Trickey

Trickey was a fisherman who lived near the mouth of the York River, close to the southernmost point in Maine. Old Trickey, as they called him (no one knew his real name), was an unusually rough and unruly character. He was an irritable and untrustworthy man who, it was said, had done devil's work during his relatively short lifetime. He was notorious as a cheat and a liar.

When he died, Old Trickey expected that the devil would reward him for a life devoted to tricking and betraying his fellow Maine fisher folk. But the devil had an unpleasant surprise for him. Trickey was cursed by his satanic master for not being quite mean enough in life, and he was condemned to remain on the coast of Maine and haul sand with a rope, an endless and futile task.

When gales blow in from the Atlantic, Old Trickey gets busy with his rope. He toils hard in stormy weather, trying to rope sand in the little coves along these rocky shores. The devil is never satisfied as

Trickey tries to move the dunes. "More sand!" commands Satan; "More rope!"

When Maine children notice that the coastal sands have been moved about, rearranged during stormy nights, their parents tell them about Old Trickey's endless work, trying to corral sand with his rope. Listen carefully when the wind is howling, children are taught. You might just hear the devil yelling at Old Trickey: "More sand! More rope!"

The Ghost of Massacre Pond

Massacre Pond, near the old town of Scarborough, just south of Portland, surely deserves its name. Not just one but two massacres occurred there in history. Both were products of the long struggle between Native Americans and the invading Europeans. These horrific massacres produced at least one ghost—and an angry, vengeful ghost at that.

Is there something evil about the place itself, that two mass murders happened there? Local people have long avoided Massacre Pond, especially at night. The pond is spooky when a mist swirls about its moonlit surface. It is then that the blood-drenched ghost of Richard "Crazy Eyes" Stonewall stalks about, looking for Indians to kill.

The story tells of a band of marauding Indians who murdered some English settlers near the little pond in the 1670s, among them Stonewall's wife and infant son. Richard Stonewall, enraged with the spirit of vengeance, promptly joined the army and made it his mission in life to kill as many Indians as possible. His fellow soldiers noted that Stonewall's eyes glowed in anticipation of killing Indians and gave him the nickname, "Crazy Eyes." When Crazy Eyes died in October 1697, he was buried, as he wished, near the pond where his family had been so foully slain. His restless ghost must have been further outraged when, in 1713, Richard Hunnewell and nineteen companions were slaughtered alongside the pond by Indians on the warpath. It is said that a few of these murderous warriors themselves were killed on the spot, not by Hunnewell and his men, but by a knife-wielding phantom that rose out of his grave during the fight.

If you see a figure with smoldering red eyes glaring at you near the pond, leave quickly. Crazy Eyes Stonewall is still on patrol.

The York Witch

It is said that a witch is buried in the Old York cemetery, and that her ghost still haunts it. But was she really a witch, or was she simply a well-meaning old woman who did her best to help her neighbors?

York, only a few miles from Kittery Point, Maine's southernmost point on the Atlantic Ocean, is one of Maine's oldest towns, incorporated in 1652. It is on the site of an even older Indian community, Agamenticus.

The cemetery is even older than the nearby church, which dates to 1747. The oldest headstones are decorated with death's-heads with wings—looking like flying skulls—and meant to symbolize the decay of the body but the immortality of the spirit or soul. Normally, a grave is marked only by a headstone. A few also have a smaller footstone to mark the other limit of the grave. But one grave, known locally as the "Witch's Grave," features both headstone and footstone and, between them, a huge boulder covering the middle of the grave.

This is the grave of Mary Miller Jason, hanged for witchcraft in 1744. The purpose of the boulder? To ensure that Mary does not rise out of her grave to haunt those who accused her. The local legend is that the massive boulder fails to seal her in her grave—that her ghost walks about the cemetery, the hangman's noose still around her neck.

At the time of Mary Miller Jason's trial, many in the community believed that she was innocent. However, in the emotionally charged atmosphere of the times, those accused of witchcraft had to prove that they were not witches, an impossibility. Mary was accused of making magic potions. Her defenders said that she had learned about natural, herbal medicines from the local Indians and only sought to help sick neighbors. Was Mary a witch or merely a pioneer in natural healing? We will never know the truth, for Mary paid with her life for living in a time when witchcraft hysteria periodically swept through New England and persecuted many defenseless old women.

If the prospect of meeting Mary's ghost isn't enough to keep you out of the cemetery at night, there also is a tradition that a flock of crows frequents her grave. Allegedly, the crows are "familiars"—

supernatural animals controlled by witches to do their bidding and help protect them. If the ghost doesn't get you, the crows will, or at least that's the story.

The Mysterious Fires of Boon Island

One of the oldest lighthouses in Maine was erected on Boon Island, near Kittery, in 1811. According to local legend, however, the Boon Island Light is hardly necessary, as a mysterious, ghostly bonfire can be seen flickering late on stormy nights on the little island.

According to tradition, the coastal trader *Increase*, which plied between Plymouth, Massachusetts, and Pemaquid, near Boothbay, was wrecked in a storm on the island in April of 1682. The survivors, three white men and an Indian, struggled ashore. Finding no sign of habitation, the castaways had given up hope of being rescued when, a month after their shipwreck, they spotted the smoke of a large fire on the mainland. This smoke turned out to be from the burnt offerings of a large gathering of Indians. It was their custom to sacrifice game animals to the flames in honor of the spirits who, thus encouraged, would ensure a bountiful harvest that fall.

The castaways gathered driftwood and built a great bonfire to attract the attention of the mainlanders, which they did. They were rescued and named the scene of their salvation Boon (a piece of good luck) Island. Is it the ghosts of these lucky castaways who build the mysterious bonfires—spectral fires that leave behind no trace of ashes?

Captain Larrabee's Duty Calls

During the early colonial period, Maine was up for grabs. Maine once belonged to France. Or, at least, the French thought so. The British, of course, strongly disagreed. Even the Dutch claimed Maine for a time. To the south lay English colonies in Massachusetts, Rhode Island, and Connecticut, all the way to Virginia, and eventually, Georgia. To the northeast lay French colonies in Acadia, later renamed Nova Scotia, New Brunswick, and Prince Edward Island.

And to the north of that was the longtime English colony of New-foundland. There was a confusion of land claims based on sketchy descriptions from many different explorers. For more than a century, Britain and France fought battles, signed peace treaties, traded territory, and went to war again over the lands between the St. Lawrence River and the southern coasts of Maine.

It was against this background of a long bitter struggle that the story of Capt. John Larrabee, and his ghost, stands out. Prouts Neck is one of hundreds of rocky promontories jutting out into the Atlantic along the coast of Maine, lying south of Portland and east of Old Orchard Beach. During the French and Indian War, a small block-house was constructed at the southern tip of the little peninsula to help protect the coast from French raiders.

The French and Indian War was called that because the French had convinced many Indian tribes that the British, always strongly expansionist, were a greater threat to Indian independence than were the French. And so it came about that 500 Frenchmen and their Indian allies besieged the little blockhouse on Prouts Neck in 1703.

Capt. John Larrabee and his eight men, who were stationed in the blockhouse, courageously held out for a week. Finally, totally out of ammunition and short on food and water, they surrendered. The captain was bitter about having to give up his blockhouse. When his general commented that Larrabee had no choice but to surrender to a superior force, the captain retorted that the French were in no way superior, just more numerous.

Although the blockhouse is long gone, the ghost of Captain Larrabee is said to still be on patrol at the site. If challenged by an apparition in soldier dress, be sure to answer in English. Woe to anyone who answers the captain in French.

The Preacher and the Cats From Hell

The little town of York Harbor has long been a fashionable resort. One reason for its justified reputation is its very wide beach, a rarity in rock-bound coastal Maine. The section known as Long Beach is one of the most attractive in the entire state. In such a sunny, carefree holiday location, one wouldn't expect to encounter the devil's minions.

The preacher at the little church in nearby York was approached by a very upset parishioner who was convinced that her house was haunted by an evil spirit. Could the preacher help by convincing the evil spirit to leave her in peace? Surely the power of good would defeat the forces of evil. The preacher could hardly refuse to confront this evil, so he agreed to spend a night alone in the house.

He brought his Bible and settled down by the fire to read. He didn't have to wait very long. The first ghost was that of a man who was holding his severed head, from which blood was dripping. "Are you going to stay until the devil comes?" asked this ghost. The preacher shuddered and began praying aloud. The first ghost then evaporated like morning mist in bright sunlight. The preacher breathed a great sigh of relief and resumed reading his Bible.

The next evil spirit appeared in the form of a wolf with glowing red eyes and blood dripping from its fangs. "Are you going to stay to meet the Prince of Darkness?" growled the specter. Trembling now in fear, his hands hardly able to hold the Good Book, the preacher began reciting the Lord's Prayer. The wolf slunk away, his shadow seeming to pass right through the door.

Next came a little black kitten. It rubbed against his leg, but sparks flew from its fur and it sprang back when the preacher tried to touch it. A larger black cat then stalked into the room, hissing and growling at the preacher. "Are you going to wait to meet the Lord of the Underworld?" asked the cat. The preacher took a wooden cross from his pocket and extended it toward the cat, which suddenly dissolved in flames, screaming.

Now there appeared a huge black panther. It snarled, showing long, sharp fangs glistening with blood. Razor-sharp claws were extended as it stalked the preacher. "So you stayed to meet Satan!" it growled as it prepared to pounce. The preacher now began the most fervent, heartfelt prayer of his life. Recalling the biblical story of Daniel in the lion's den, he asked God to protect him as he had protected Daniel. The crouching panther screamed in pain as a silver arrow seemed to leap out of the preacher's Bible, slicing into the beast's heart. The panther's body glowed like molten metal, and then it was gone. The preacher fainted and was discovered the next

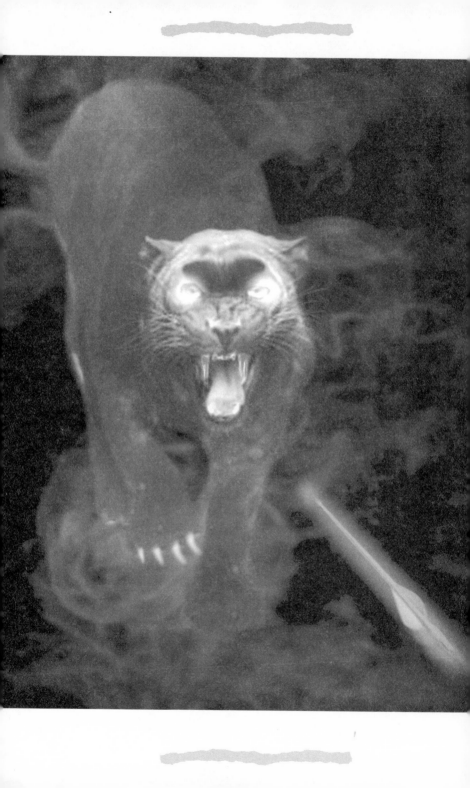

morning in a deep sleep, his hands clutching his Bible. "What a fantastic nightmare I had!" he said. "At least, I pray it was a dream." He served his church long and honorably, but never again talked about the night he met the cats from hell.

Inspected by a UFO

If unidentified flying objects are carrying alien beings from outer space, just why are they here on planet Earth? Many students of UFOs think that the aliens are here on scientific missions. They are curious about life on Earth and are studying us. Many encounters with UFOs, for example, involve the kidnapping of people, at least temporarily, into a spacecraft where they are probed and examined like laboratory specimens.

Other theories about UFOs are that they are carrying vacationing aliens from other solar systems on a tour of odd and interesting planets in far off galaxies. "See five continents in five days! Witness weird Earth-creatures in their native habitats!"

Maybe aliens smart enough to build UFOs with their amazing flight capabilities are doing both scientific surveys and a little sightseeing. That is the impression of two teenagers who had a briefly terrifying, but ultimately harmless encounter with a UFO.

This happened in the 1950s, but the two teens waited until only recently when, as an elderly married couple, they decided to go public with their story. The incident occurred on a lonely back road, a lover's lane in fall, near the town of Saco.

Every community has a lover's lane; Saco was no exception. The teens were eager for a little privacy in which to get to know each other more intimately. Of course, they weren't supposed to be there at all—a factor in why they waited so long to tell their tale. The cover story was that they had gone to see a movie in town. The young man had read a rather lengthy review of the movie, and they discussed it in case there were any parental questions about the film.

No sooner had the young couple made their way through the preliminaries and were about to "head for home base," when they realized, to their great surprise and horror, that they were not alone. A brilliant white light suddenly flooded the interior of the car. The car radio, which had been softly playing the romantic music of Frank Sinatra, went dead, as did the front dashboard lights. There was a very low, barely audible humming sound, as though from some electrical apparatus. Both young people experienced what seemed like a body-temperature oily liquid enveloping their bodies, moving downward from head to feet. The sensation, not unpleasant, lasted only for a few seconds, then disappeared with no trace of moisture or residue. Next, what looked like a large pane of transparent, greenish glass seemed to flow over their bodies, much like the visual sensation of the medical body scans developed by human scientists fifty years later.

Finally, as though the aliens' scientific scan of the teenage couple was complete, the bright light faded out. Then, through the windshield, they could see a huge, cigar-shaped UFO, outlined in lights that were blinking rapidly, hovering above their car. It accelerated suddenly, quickly disappearing in the night sky.

Badly shaken but unhurt, the couple decided to keep this experience secret. One tiny detail, however, was hard to explain. The boy's brand new wristwatch had stopped and would not work again. A local jeweler, asked to examine the watch, which was still under warranty, said that it was not the fault of the manufacturer. "You must have carelessly exposed the watch to a very powerful electromagnetic field," he said. "It will never work again." A frozen watch was a small price to pay for a frightening, but otherwise harmless UFO encounter, figured the couple, who went on to marry, raise a family, and, of course, keep a secret for half a century.

A Tale of Davy Jones

Among old-time sailors, the name Davy Jones is associated with death and evil spirits. The bottom of the sea often is referred to as "Davy Jones' Locker," and is the abode of the ghosts of drowned sailors.

It is really not known where the name Davy Jones came from originally, or how it became associated with supernatural evil, but there are a few theories on the matter. Some believe that "Davy" is a West Indies voodoo name for the devil. The Welsh surname Jones may have been derived from the biblical name Jonah—a name that, for obvious reasons, never should be given to a future seaman or fisherman.

More than two centuries ago, though, sailors on the Maine coast had their own version of a "Davy Jones" story. Around 1740 a slave ship out of Liverpool was transporting a boatload of slaves from the Caribbean to the American colonies.

The slave ship *Albatross* was captained by Henry Scott, a man of notably bad temper. He took a particular dislike to one of his crew, a stout, elderly man called David "Davy" Jones. Davy always was slow moving, and this enraged Captain Scott, who liked his men to literally jump to attention when given orders. Davy not only moved slowly, he had an insolent habit of muttering under his breath whenever the captain spoke to him.

Finally, their simmering anger boiled over. A sudden squall blew up and the captain ordered all hands to climb up the rigging and take in the sails lest a strong gust shred the sails or even rip down the masts. The ship was in danger, and Davy Jones remained seated on deck, defying the captain's orders.

Enraged beyond words, the captain went down to his cabin, fetched his flintlock pistol, and shot Davy. As Davy Jones lay dying on the deck, he said to the captain, "You have done for me, but I will never leave you." And with that curse, he died. As was the custom, Davy's body was sewn into a canvas sail, weighted, and dispatched overboard. The captain refused to have any burial services read. No hymns were sung. Davy was simply dumped overboard, which the crew regarded as a very bad omen.

As he had threatened with his dying breath, Davy didn't leave the ship, or the captain. The crew talked among themselves about seeing Davy's ghost on board. Davy's phantom joined them at meals and drank his share of grog, too.

The captain also saw Davy. Davy's spirit perched at the foot of Captain Scott's bed and pulled the covers off whenever the captain began to drop off to sleep. When the exhausted, sleepless captain tried to eat or drink, Davy would knock away the plate or goblet. Whenever the captain walked on deck, Davy was there to trip him up and send him sprawling.

At long last, the captain called the crew together. Utterly exhausted and ceaselessly tormented by Davy Jones's evil spirit, the Captain announced that the first mate would sail *Albatross* into the nearest port, Kittery, while the captain left the ship to escape the ghost. Captain Scott was lowered overboard in a small boat. No sooner had the boat pulled away from the ship, when there was a terrifying scream from the captain. "He's here in the boat with me!" he screamed, "I'm truly doomed!" With that, both boat and captain sank beneath the waves to be seen no more.

The Haunted Bracelet

Can inanimate objects communicate knowledge of the future? Or, more likely, can they somehow be used by the dead to communicate with loved ones still alive? A resident of Kennebunkport, recently deceased, was convinced that her dead husband was using a bracelet, a Christmas gift he had given her shortly before he died, as a means of warning her from the spirit world.

The bracelet was of silver links with silver charms dangling from it—a style very popular in the 1960s. Among these charms were a heart, an angel, a cupid with bow and arrow, and a medallion with an amethyst, the wife's birthstone. The angel was a messenger from heaven, or the spirit world. Cupid represented the wife's love for others in her immediate family, while the birthstone was a symbol of herself. The heart was her heart, which could be vulnerable to much emotional pain as she was so sensitive to other people's troubles.

The woman especially treasured her silver charm bracelet, being her husband's final gift to her. Naturally, she kept it well polished, a chore made easier by keeping the bracelet in an airtight plastic bag while not wearing it. Some months following her husband's untimely death, the gleaming silver charm bracelet's angel, cupid, and heart suddenly turned black with heavy tarnish. The rest of the bracelet remained shining bright. The next day, the woman learned that a favorite cousin had suffered a fatal heart attack. Had the charm bracelet foretold a tragedy?

Early one morning, as the woman was fastening the clasp of her bracelet, the angel and heart both blackened before her eyes. As she frantically applied silver polish, the angel and heart tarnished again immediately. A few hours later, the news broke about a terrible disaster in New York. The date was September 11, 2001.

Now the woman lived in awe of her future-foretelling bracelet. She stopped wearing it, keeping it sealed in the airtight bag in an attempt to keep its charms always bright and free of the foreboding tarnish. She asked her family to be certain that, when the time came, the bracelet would be buried with her. She wanted to spare her family the pain of advance news of tragedy.

One morning, the woman glanced apprehensively at the bracelet, still in its protective plastic bag. She fainted immediately and soon was dead of a cerebral hemorrhage. The angel and birthstone charms were black with tarnish. The bracelet, freshly polished, was placed in her casket as she had requested. A glimpse into the future can be a mixed blessing.

Greater Portland

THE PORTLAND AREA INCLUDES MAINE'S LARGEST CITY, ITS SUBURBS, and near neighbors. This compact region includes the coastline from Prouts Neck to Harpswell and the many islands of Casco Bay.

Jane Comes Home to Stay

An old house in Portland was recently demolished to make way for a highway-widening project. Although it was a solidly built house, perhaps it is just as well that it is gone, for the house came with an unusual tenant—an old skull. Whenever the house changed hands, the new owners were convinced, one way or another, to keep the skull in the house. The alternative was a spiteful ghost who would make the house a nightmare for its occupants until the skull was restored to its rightful place in the house.

Almost two centuries ago, three maiden sisters inherited a whaling fortune from their father. They decided to build a handsome new house in which they'd all live. They planned it down to the last doorknob and hired the very best workmen. Their dream house was finished and furnished and decorated in the latest fashion. Delighted, the sisters moved in and began enjoying the new home. "I never want to leave!" declared Jane, the eldest.

But fate cut short her pleasure in her new home. She met a pair of beggars in the street one winter evening while returning from a social event, and they asked for a few coins. She opened her purse intending to give them enough for a hot meal, as she was of a generous spirit. One of the men noticed a large diamond sparkling on her hand. Suddenly, the situation turned ugly. "We'll have that ring, too!" one muttered. Jane refused angrily, saying it was a family heirloom of sentimental value. Frustrated, the beggars knocked her down and delivered a vicious kick to her head.

Poor Jane was carried to her home, stunned and bleeding from every opening in her head. As she lay dying, she made what her sisters thought was a delirious and rather gruesome last request. She said that she never wanted to leave the lovely new house she had so looked forward to occupying with her siblings. "Let my body be buried but keep my head here in the house," she begged. To ease Jane's last moments, her sisters agreed rather than argue with her, though they had no intention of keeping such a bizarre promise.

In due time, Jane was buried. All of her. Then trouble began.

Very late on the evening of Jane's burial, the surviving sisters heard a loud knocking at the door. It was persistent and could not be ignored. But when the door was opened, there was no one to be seen. The sisters, puzzled and annoyed, went back to bed. Again, a loud commotion at their door brought them down from bed. No one was there. Annoyance turned to fear. Who, or what, was knocking on the door? Why wouldn't they, or it, go away?

The nightly pounding on the front door not only continued, but things got worse. Windows left closed, and locked, were found open in the morning. The bed in Jane's bedroom just would not stay properly made up—the bed covers were disarrayed during the night, as though a very restless sleeper had occupied the bed.

Then a truly frightening apparition began to move about the house—an image of Jane, carrying her own head in her hands. Terrified by now, the sisters remembered their hasty, insincere agreement with their dying sister's last request. Jane's coffin was unearthed. When the lid was pried back, it was seen that the corpse held its head on its chest. The skull appeared to be grinning.

Jane's skull was placed in an elaborately carved hatbox and installed in her former bedroom. Nights from then on were peacefully uneventful. No more midnight knockings on the door. No more ghosts holding their own head in front of them.

Later owners of the house learned that attempts to rebury Jane's skull would produce nightly disturbances at the front door and visits from Jane's ghost. When Jane's skull was returned to the house, all was quiet once again.

Jane really didn't want to leave. And heaven help anyone who tried to evict her.

The Steamship Portland's Passengers Come Home

Longtime Portland residents report a strange sight that seems to occur every November 27—the anniversary of a famous tragedy. Ghostly figures approach the old port exchange near Portland's docks. They are dressed warmly in old fashioned Victorian-style clothing: long overcoats, hats, scarves, and gloves. But their clothing is soaking wet, and bits of seaweed cling to their sodden garments. Nearly half of them are children. The massive Victorian port exchange was once the place to obtain information about ships, especially overdue ships. Whenever a ship was reported lost or overdue, relatives and friends of crew or passengers would gather at the port exchange to share news and hope for a reunion with the missing.

November 27 is the anniversary of the day that the steamship *Portland* went missing way back in 1898. Are the victims of the storm still looking for a ghostly reunion with their loved ones? Are these spirits restless because they were never recovered from the cruel sea, their bodies never buried in proper graves?

Many refer to the *Portland* as Maine's *Titanic*—both famous disasters at sea that cost many lives. There is an eerie parallel in the stories of the *Titanic* and the *Portland*. In both cases, the ship's captains were warned about potential danger to their ships. In both cases, the warnings were ignored, and the ships were lost. However, at least in the case of the *Titanic*, over 700 of her 2,227 crew and passengers were saved. No one survived the sinking of the *Portland*.

The SS *Portland*, built in Bath, Maine, was a sidewheeler—seemingly an odd choice for an ocean-going ship in the late 1890s. She had been designed to navigate shallow rivers as well as the Atlantic—a design flaw that may well have contributed to her tragic end, for she had a shallow draft and consequently tended to roll badly in heavy seas. At 2,253 tons, the 280-foot-long ship was not exactly small, but she was not built for rough seas.

When the *Portland* was lost with all souls aboard, blame was placed on her captain's stubborn refusal to heed warnings about the weather, just as *Titanic*'s sinking was blamed on her captain's failing to slow down on news about icebergs ahead. Capt. Hollis Blanchard routinely checked in with the weather bureau in Boston before returning to Portland. Although, of course, weather forecasters of the day did not have radar or satellite images of the weather, they did have telegraphed reports from weather stations across the country. They knew, and informed Captain Blanchard, that a strong blizzard was approaching from the west toward New England. According to stories circulated after the disaster, Captain Blanchard decided to take the risk because his holiday-bound passengers were eager to get to Portland, and the Captain's own daughter was having a Thanksgiving party at his home there.

The Thanksgiving storm on that fated voyage produced 40- and 50-foot waves according to coastal observers. The *Portland* must have capsized before any lifeboats could be launched. Those aboard never had a chance. Is it any wonder that their restless spirits still haunt the Portland waterfront, which they never saw again in life?

A History Lesson from a Ghost

Three words from the lips of a ghost once started a local Portland boy on the path to a successful career as a historian, but no one ever actually heard these three words.

Men of Maine responded with enthusiasm to President Abraham Lincoln's call for troops. Maine folks had always been opposed to the evil institution of slavery, and the Pine Tree State contributed far more than its share of the "boys in blue" who finally defeated the Confederacy. Portland alone sent 5,000 of its sons into battle—an astounding 20 percent of its population at the time.

Of course, this meant that many brave Maine soldiers and sailors lost their lives in the conflict, their bodies returned to lie in honored graves across the state. One of these courageous dead once gave a brief, but impressive history lesson to a young boy, a lesson that shaped his life.

In the early years of the twentieth century, it was the custom of a local Portland family to visit the graves of family members on Memorial Day, especially the grave of an ancestor who'd died fighting in the Civil War. In those days, Memorial Day was known as Decoration Day, meaning that the graves of war veterans were decorated with bright, new American flags and, of course, fresh flowers.

This family had risen very early in order to decorate their family plot before going on the traditional picnic. Their young boy, we'll call him Jack, wandered off a bit by himself, as boys will. He came across a strange but somehow not frightening sight. The apparition of a Union officer sat perched on his own gravestone. The ghost appeared to be very sad, shaking his head slowly in sorrow and regret. His lips moved, though no sound was heard. Now Jack, hard of hearing since birth, had trained himself in reading lips. The ghost had mouthed the words, "seventy in seven." What could that possibly mean? Why were those odd words so important to the ghost of the Union officer slain in battle?

No one would believe Jack about seeing the ghost, much less speculate on the meaning of the spirit's cryptic message. Jack's interest in Civil War history became so compelling that he went to college and then graduate school to pursue his interest. One day, he told his ghost story to a sympathetic professor. "Was the dead officer a member of the 1st Maine Heavy Artillery?" asked the professor. "Yes, but why is that important?" was Jack's reply. "Because," said his teacher, "the 1st Maine sustained a record number of casualties at the Battle of Petersburg, Virginia, on June 18, 1864, when they lost 635 out of a total of 900 men in just 7 minutes." "That accounts for the 'in seven' from the lips of the officer's ghost, but what about the 'seventy'"? "Do the math," was the reply, "635 casualties out of 900 men is almost exactly a 70 percent loss."

"Seventy in seven." Everyone hopes that this is a tragic record that will never be broken.

The Triton Who Drowned the Sailor

Many a sailor and fisherman have drowned in Casco Bay, but only one is said to have been deliberately killed by a triton or merman. Sailors may look forward to seeing a bedazzling mermaid, but a merman is another thing entirely. Mermen, or tritons, are said to be the sons of Poseidon, the Greek god of the sea (the Romans called him Neptune). Half man and half fish, tritons are not always friendly to mortals. Tritons sound trumpets made of conch shells; the mournful wail of a triton's conch sounds much like a foghorn, but can be terrifying to anyone who has had an unpleasant encounter with a triton.

Peak's Island in Casco Bay is just two miles from downtown Portland. It once was owned by Michael Mitton, son-in-law of Portland's first settler, George Cleeve. According to legend, Michael was out alone fishing in his dory when a triton swam up to his boat. Michael tried to fend off the monster with an oar, but the triton grasped hold of the side of the dory. Afraid that the triton could capsize the little boat, Michael seized a hatchet and, with one mighty blow, severed both hands of this son of Poseidon.

To his horror, Michael Mitton saw that the monster's hands remained fastened to his boat. He could not pry them loose. It was then that Mike heard the haunting sound of the triton's conch, and at the sound, the severed hands gave one mighty effort at rocking his boat, finally flipping him into the water and swamping the dory. Michael drowned that day.

To this day, when Maine sailors hear the conch trumpet of triton, they head for land at full speed. No one wants to meet an angry triton.

Cliff Island's "Wrecker" Ghost

On Cliff Island, off Portland in Casco Bay, they tell the tale of the wrecker who was condemned to walk the shoreline for eternity as penance for his foul misdeeds.

Captain Keiff was an outlaw—a smuggler, pirate, and a wrecker. Wreckers were heartless murderers and thieves who lured ships to destruction and then salvaged their cargoes. The favored technique was to lead a horse along the beach on a stormy night. Tied to the horse's tail was a lighted lantern. To sailors at sea, the swinging light looked like a ship's riding light, signifying a safe shipping channel when in fact, only rocks lay in wait for unwary ships.

Captain Keiff grew rich by salvaging the cargoes of his victims. Supposedly, he buried the bodies that washed ashore in his front lawn, an area still known as Keiff's Garden.

When the evil wrecker died, his spirit was condemned to lead a phantom horse, lantern swinging from its tail, along the rocky shores of Cliff Island. The ghost of Captain Keiff must wander alone in the icy spray and bitter winds of winter gale, endlessly patrolling the shore with his false signals of safety. The ghost must be frustrated by the fact that, despite his repeated efforts, the lantern will not stay lit. No other ship ever will be lured into danger by Keiff's lantern.

Haskell Island's Rats and Cats

Haskell Island, near Harpswell on Casco Bay, is said to have been the scene of bewitched animals: first rats, and then cats.

Everyone knows that animals frequently behave differently in large groups than when they are alone. Similarly, people in mobs don't behave as they would individually.

Witches often have companion animals, called their "familiars." These animals have been bewitched to help the witches carry out their evil deeds. These familiars are commissioned by the devil to protect the witch. Many animals, even insects, have been accused of being witches' familiars, but the most common animal henchmen are said to be cats, rats, and toads.

Haskell Island has witnessed what amounted to occupying armies of first rats and then cats. Nearly two centuries ago, a lone lobsterman lived on the island. The little island was literally overrun by rats, which, it is believed, swam ashore from a sinking ship. The lobsterman, old John Humphrey, seemed unfazed by the rats that swarmed over the island. "They just eat old bait from my bait barrel," he reassured friends. "They don't bother me."

One day, however, fishermen from nearby Harpswell noticed that no smoke was rising from Humphrey's chimney. Nor could they see any activity around the old man's waterside shack. They rowed out to investigate. When they opened the door, they were met by a squealing swarm of huge rats. As they entered the cabin, they saw, to their horror, that John Humphrey had been reduced to a jumble of gnawed bones on his bed. The lobsterman had been eaten by the army of rats.

The people of Harpswell were determined to avenge John Humphrey. They descended on Haskell Island armed with clubs and guns and exterminated the rodents, or tried to, for visitors to the island that following year found rats again roaming everywhere.

Haskell Island was avoided by people due to its bad reputation, until, that is, two brothers from the mainland decided to take back the island from the rats.

Wallace and Bruce Mills set up a lobstering enterprise on Haskell, bringing with them a dozen of the biggest, meanest alley cats they could find. A war was on. At first, it was an uphill battle for the aggressive felines, but the cats prevailed. Soon, not a rat was to be seen. The cats multiplied, but the Mills brothers never succeeded in giving away kittens, as this island race of cats were never cute or cuddly. They were born hostile, aggressive, and hungry. After the rats were all dispatched, the cats moved on to birds. Songbirds disappeared. Even seagulls, normally the fearless bandits of the shoreline, learned not to land on Haskell Island. The Mills brothers began spending more time catching fish to feed the ever-larger cat population than they did attending to their lobster pots.

If strangers attempted to land on the island, they were frightened off by a yowling mob of hyperactive cats, teeth bared and claws flared. Eventually, other fishermen noticed that the Mills brothers had not been seen for weeks. No one was foolhardy enough to land amidst the pack of enraged, hungry, half-wild cats. Finally, someone ventured close enough to Haskell to toss ashore some poisoned fish. Scores of cat carcasses soon littered the shore—a feast for the seagulls who returned to reclaim Haskell.

It was decades before anyone was brave enough to settle once more on Haskell Island. There are no rats on Haskell Island to this day; nor are there any cats. Did rats and cats there once revert to a more primitive, violently aggressive way of life because they were isolated on a small island? Or was Haskell Island cursed?

The Dead Ship of Harpswell

They used to tell this tale around the now-forgotten town of Harpswell, which no longer appears on most maps. It was near South Harpswell, on Casco Bay north of Portland. On foggy days, of which there are many along the Maine coast, fishermen at sea would see what looked like the skeleton of a great wooden sailing vessel. This apparition's huge timber frame showed through her rotted hull like the bones of a decaying corpse poking through rotting flesh.

Although great gaps appeared in the ship's worn and frayed sheathing, no seawater invaded her ragged sides: This was a dead ship, for while she sailed on, reappearing time after time out on the bay, she displayed no name. No flag flew from her tall masts, which held tattered shreds of sails—sails that nonetheless billowed out in a wind and propelled the dead ship onward. No sailors ever were seen aboard. The mystery ship never made a sound as she sailed right past the awestruck fisherman—no creak of timbers nor flap of sails. Ominously, there was no spray off her bow as she cut through the waves, no ripple at her stern, nor even any wake left at her passing. Although no helmsman stands behind her wheel, she skillfully avoids any rocks or reefs in her path, never grounding, though she sails close to shore sometimes.

What is the dead ship's purpose, its mission? Why does this phantom ship appear out on the water only just before a death onshore? Is the dreaded dead ship bringing the Angel of Death across the waters? Or is she arriving just in time to ferry the departing spirits of the dead on their journey to another world? Once, and only once so goes the legend, did a fishing boat dare to cut across the bows of the dead ship. Although the seas were calm and the boat's crew experienced, the fishing boat quickly disappeared in a sudden whirlpool. There were no survivors, so stay well away from the dead ship, if you are so unlucky as to see her.

Making a Desert in Maine

A dozen or so miles north of Portland, near the little town of Freeport, lies a mysterious patch of sand dunes known as the Desert of Maine. It's a tourist attraction, conveniently close to Interstate 95 and near to Maine's biggest city. This desert looks as though it should be in Arizona, the Sahara, or California's famed Death Valley. High sand dunes and thirty-foot-deep gullies spread over nearly 1,000 acres, surrounded by green pastures and the lush forests typical of the Pine Tree State. Why is there a miniature Sahara close to the coast of such a well-watered, forested state?

Scientists think they know why it's there, but ghost hunters have a different explanation. Geologists believe that this little ocean of sand originated in the bed of an ancient glacial lake. The very fine sand, so readily blown by the wind into steep dunes that slowly move out over the surrounding green terrain, sparkles in the sun. This glittery powder, according to geologists, was pulverized when a giant sheet of ice ground across the rough gray rocks once containing shiny sheets of mica.

There is an old tradition in the neighborhood, however, that the desert in the midst of greenery is the product of ghostly vengeance. Both the scientists and the believers in ghosts agree that the desert was not always there. In the colonial period, this area was productive farmland, not a sandy waste. The story goes that in 1797, a man named Thomas Grayson bought a 300-acre farm on the spot. The farm prospered. Thomas suddenly was stricken with a fatal disease. With no time to write a will, he asked his second wife to promise him that the farm would go to David, his son by his first wife. She agreed, but when Thomas was safely buried, she handed the property over to her own son by a previous marriage. There was nothing Thomas could do about her treachery from the grave. Or was there?

Years after Thomas Grayson's death, a small circle of sand appeared in the midst of a field. It grew steadily, expanding outward like the widening lens of a camera. There are those who swear that they saw the ghostly figure of a man in the swirling sands blown by the wind, as the dunes marched across formerly productive land.

Did Thomas Grayson reach out from the grave to curse the heir to his farm who was not his own flesh and blood? Is the desert of Maine a result of ghostly vengeance? Many still believe so.

Don't Bother a Treasure Seeker

Among the many places along Maine's coast where pirates are said to have buried treasure is Great Chebeague Island in Casco Bay. Great Chebeague is within sight of Portland and is the second largest island in the bay. Unlike many of Maine's coastal islands, which tend to be rocky with steep cliffs plunging into the sea, Great Chebeague has many fine white sand beaches. These beaches are the delight of vacationers, and they present easy access from the sea for sailors wishing to land.

There is an old story about a local young man who was cursed for his persistence in trying to help a treasure hunter. Or was he, as the treasure seeker believed, trying to help himself to the pirate's trove? There long had been rumors of buried pirate gold on Great Chebeague, but then it seems that many islands on this coast have legends of pirate loot.

If there were buried treasure on Great Chebeague, it would not be easy to find without a map, as the island is over 2,000 acres in extent. But someone did have some clues.

One winter day, as the wind was howling through the island's pine and spruce trees, an old man, a stranger, showed up. He told people that he was the sole survivor of a ship's crew that had been captured by pirates many years before. The kidnapped sailors had been forced, at sword point, to dig several holes on Great Chebeague, and then were taken back to their ship anchored offshore. Several of the pirates remained behind on the island for a few hours before rejoining the ship.

The captive sailors figured that the crafty pirates had forced them to dig several wave holes so that, afterward, the outlaws could choose one in which to bury their loot. The diggers would not know which of their many excavations was chosen to receive the treasure chest, and so could not easily find it.

The old man told the islanders that, if they did not interfere with his digging around the area, he would split the treasure with the community before he left. Everyone but one young fellow went along with this proposition.

This islander stalked the old sailor, repeatedly offering his help in digging. He wouldn't take no for an answer and made a pest of himself. The old man marked off his latest dig site with a rope, and begged the islanders looking on to stay outside the rope. Again, the eager would-be-assistant stepped over the rope.

At this, the old sailor cried out to the group of onlookers, "I call on God and you people to witness that within a year, this young fool will be tied in knots even as I could tie the rope." And, sure enough, soon afterward, the young fool was drenched in cold water when he mysteriously fell off his boat. Shivering uncontrollably, he was confined to bed with an agonizing illness that contorted his arms and legs. When he died, it was necessary to break his bones in order to properly fit him into his casket. It is curious that the corpse screamed during the bone breaking.

What about the old treasure hunter? Absorbed in the tragic spectacle of the young fool "tied in knots" in his deathbed, the islanders forgot about him. He was never seen again, nor was any treasure.

Still Arguing

Right in the heart of Portland lies the Old Eastern Cemetery. Only six acres in size, it is a very crowded cemetery. It also is a very haunted cemetery. Among many alleged ghosts, two stand out, for they seem to be engaged in an eternal argument.

The two phantoms are dressed in the uniforms of naval officers, but one uniform is American, and the other British. They roar at one another unintelligibly, gesturing angrily. Clearly, it is a heated argument. Their midnight confrontations always end abruptly if a living soul approaches, at which time the contenders simply evaporate from their perches atop their tombstones.

In life, they were enemies, and they both died fighting one another during the War of 1812. One of that war's most decisive naval battles took place off Monhegan on September 5, 1813, when the U.S. *Enterprise* engaged the British *Boxer*. Lt. William Burrows commanded *Enterprise*. Capt. Samuel Blyth was in command of *Boxer*. It was a furious battle at close quarters, during which both commanders were killed. *Enterprise* won and brought the defeated British ship into Portland as a prize of war. The two gallant commanders were buried side by side with full military honors.

But each finds it difficult to rest in peace buried next to his opponent. The argument goes on still.

Portland's Treasure Island

Little Jewell Island is one of the outermost islands in Casco Bay, the location of Maine's largest city, Portland. Although the island is named for its first non-Indian owner, George Jewell, its name came to have another meaning, that of precious stones, to the local Portlanders.

Somehow the rumor got started that the famous pirate, Captain Kidd, had buried treasure on Jewell. Many fortune hunters came to Jewell, hopes high and shovel in hand. The island soon was pockmarked with empty holes—the results of energetic digging.

A local legend grew of a mysterious stranger who arrived on Jewell Island during a January 1701 blizzard, a storm that had sent most treasure-seekers home to a cozy fireside. The stranger persuaded a local skipper to help him look for Captain Kidd's buried treasure chest.

The evidence that the stranger did find something lay in the sudden prosperity of the skipper who was enlisted in the search, and in a large hole on the beach in which lay a skeleton. The formerly poor skipper acquired a splendid new house, paying for it with Spanish gold coins. His wife took to wearing fine jewelry as she rode around town in a new carriage. Why this sudden wealth? The skipper refused to talk about it. As for the skeleton in the deep hole, that was taken as a sure sign of a pirate's "hidey-hole" for treasure. Traditionally, a sailor was killed on the spot of a treasure burial. Supposedly, his ghost would curse the treasure, protecting it from thieves.

In any event, Jewell Island became the site of an ever more frenzied treasure hunt. Persistent treasure hunters employed divining rods in their efforts. Some sacrificed animals to encourage the spirit world to help locate treasure. People with supposed "second sight" were brought out to the island in the superstitious hope that they would find the gold and jewels that were believed still hidden.

There are those who swear more than two centuries after Captain Kidd was hanged in London that mysterious lights can still be seen on Jewell Island late at night. Are ghostly treasure seekers still active? Why do freshly dug holes still appear on the island's shores when no one will admit digging them?

The Ghost Who Started a War

As is well known in ghost lore, ghosts commonly originate in violent and untimely deaths. Such a ghost was born at the hands of unspeakably callous and cruel drunken English sailors.

The town of Saco is one of the oldest in Maine. Saco, south of Portland, is located in an area first explored by the English in 1616. By 1624, a permanent settlement had been established. At first, relations between the English and the Native Americans were fair—no better or worse than usual. Then an ugly incident occurred that, quite literally, started a war and produced a tragic little ghost.

It was not all that unusual at the time for Europeans to regard Native Americans as a subspecies of humanity. Perhaps psychologically, it justified their arrogant treatment of Indians to believe that they were inherently inferior, little more than animals.

In 1675, a group of English sailors was rowing out on the river. Along came an Indian woman and her infant in a canoe. The sailors, much the worse for heavy drinking, decided to test the theory that, like animals, much Indian behavior was instinctive. For example, Europeans thought that Indian babies swam from birth by instinct.

The sailors deliberately upset the Indian canoe, determined to test the theory. The Indian mother succeeded in rescuing her infant and made it to shore. However, the little child died a few days afterward as a result of exposure in the chill waters. Unfortunately for all the English in the vicinity, the child's father was Squando, an Indian chief. Outraged, Squando led a series of retaliatory raids against English settlements. It was a war, a war started by sheer cruelty.

It is said that for years afterward, the wailing sound of a terrified infant could be heard out in the river when there was no one there. Were the phantom baby's cries a reminder to recognize the humanity of us all, regardless of race or ethnicity?

The Guardian Spirit of Portland Head Light

Not all ghosts are of the scary Halloween tradition. Many ghosts are benign, even benevolent. Many ghost watchers recognize a category of spirits called guardian ghosts. These phantoms appear when danger threatens or duty calls. Their protection may extend to a relative or friend, a family, or even, patriotically, an entire country. Guardian ghosts are very loyal to their duties and responsibilities. A fine example of such a guardian ghost was the spirit that once kept Portland Head Light lit even though the lighthouse keeper had been dead for a week.

Portland Head Light, built in 1791, is the oldest lighthouse on the coast of Maine. Its conical white tower rises 101 feet above high water, with a flashing light to guide ships to safe harbor at the exit of the Fore River into Casco Bay.

Early in the nineteenth century, the light was tended by a father and then his son, and possibly his grandson. It was not uncommon for the profession of lighthouse keeper to become a family tradition, handed down from father to son.

The founder of this particular dynasty was one Jacob Lancaster, a man of great dedication to his duty. Being a keeper of a lighthouse in the old days was a very demanding job. Early lights actually were big oil lamps, with whale oil the preferred fuel. Tending the light meant hauling cans of whale oil up 150 steps to the top of the tower. Several times a night, the wick needed to be trimmed to keep the guiding light burning bright. A daily chore was cleaning and polishing the glass lens and reflector. It was anything but an easy job and lives depended on it being done well and continuously—no days off for a light tender.

In due time, old Jacob passed the job on to his son, Samuel. Sam proudly carried on the tradition. The all-important light never dimmed or died under his care. His son, Sam Junior, or "Little Sam," eventually would take responsibility for the light. "Duty" and "honor" were more than just words in the Lancaster household. Little Sam grew up with a great pride in the role of lighthouse keeper, very much aware of the awesome responsibilities of helping to prevent disastrous shipwrecks. "A mighty fine boy," was his father's boast.

But then, tragedy struck. At the age of twelve, Sam Junior died of typhoid. His widowed father could not bear to have his only son buried in a distant cemetery, a place he could seldom visit due to the demands of his duties at the lighthouse. Little Sam was placed in a grave by the side of the lighthouse, where his grieving father could keep the plot neatly tended and surrounded by flowers.

And then old Sam fell mortally ill. As luck would have it, it was during a winter northeaster, when gale-force winds drove pounding surf against the rocky shore and black clouds blotted out the moon and stars at night. The dying lighthouse keeper couldn't mount the stairs to attend to his duty.

But the light shone brightly nonetheless. The Portland Head Light functioned perfectly for an entire week after Sam's death, until a friend came to check up on Sam, who had been "feeling poorly," as he put it. The mystery of the light continuing to flash while its keeper

lay dead in the cottage below was solved finally. Several sea captains reported seeing the figure of a boy waving reassuringly at them from the lighthouse's "hurricane deck," the iron catwalk at the top of the light, as their ships passed nearby. That boy could only have been the spirit of Little Sam, seeing to it that the light never failed.

Making the Ghost Whole Again

How do the living deal with ghosts? Ghosts can make life unpleasant—indeed, almost unbearable. A haunted house is no joke, but how does one persuade the ghost to give up its haunts and move on?

There is a legend about how a ghost was persuaded to leave the house it was haunting in Falmouth and return to its grave—a grave that was 3,000 miles away, across the Atlantic. And just why would the ghost of an English sailor, whose body lay in a churchyard back in England, haunt a house in Falmouth, Maine?

The story of the one-legged ghost of Falmouth begins with an act of British treachery and vandalism during the early days of America's struggle for independence. A British sea captain happened to be in the town of Falmouth when anti-British riots broke out. Capt. Henry Mowatt, commanding His Majesty's ship *Canceau* was arrested and accused of spying on the American rebels. Mowatt denied spying and successfully argued for his release on parole, promising to return for trial when requested. He returned all right, but not by request. He returned with a small fleet and rewarded the townspeople for their leniency and trust by ordering the citizens to abandon the town: He was about to destroy Falmouth by cannon fire. The people fled, and Mowatt's fleet opened fire, destroying 414 buildings, leveling the town. Amazingly, no Americans were killed. When a group of British sailors landed to survey the damage, though, irate patriots opened fire from the ruins. One sailor, Henry Reed, the future ghost, took a bullet in the leg. The ship's surgeon amputated the badly damaged leg on the spot to save Reed's life. The leg was tossed into a hastily dug hole near the water's edge as the British retreated back to their ships. In the course of time, a house was unknowingly built over the location of the abandoned limb. When Henry Reed died back in England years later, the trouble began.

The apparition of a one-legged man, hobbling along on a crude wooden peg leg, began to haunt the house. The occupants heard the thud of the peg leg on the stairs and across the floors late at night. Doors and windows opened and closed at random. In the morning, it could be seen that heavy furniture had been moved across the room. The nightly appearances by the ghost began to include loud laments. "My leg—I must have my leg!" mourned the ghost.

Unnerved, the house's owners moved out, then tried to rent the house to others. No tenants survived more than a few nights. The owners were persuaded to hire a local medium to hold a seance in the haunted house. Maybe the ghost would give its reasons for the haunting; perhaps it could be persuaded to leave. Sure enough, the ghost communicated with the living during the seance. It sought only to retrieve the long-missing leg so that its ghostly form would once again be whole. Only then could the spirit rest in peace.

The house's owner agreed to help dig up the cellar floor to locate the remains of the severed leg. The ghost, a greenish, glowing fog-like image, hovered near as the floor was dug up. Finally, the shovel unearthed a few bones. Frozen by fear, the speechless homeowner watched as the phosphorescent image of the amputated leg, freed from its grave, rose up and merged with the ghost of its owner. Like a fog evaporating in the morning sun the ghost disappeared, never to be seen or heard from again. At least not in Falmouth.

Central Coast

THIS EXTENSIVE REGION RUNS ALONG MAINE'S COAST FROM THE VICINITY of Boothbay Harbor to the famous retreat of the super rich, Bar Harbor. The Central Shore includes many of the larger islands off Maine's coastline.

The Ghost that Toasts Independence

The Goose River bridge in Rockport is haunted. Patriotic Americans need have no fear of the ghost, however. All the ghost wants is to have you join him in a tankard of ale, drinking a toast to the independence of the United States.

At the time of the American Revolution, the present town of Rockport on Penobscot Bay near Camden was known as Goose River. The coast of Maine was hit hard by the Revolutionary War. Most Mainers lived on the coast, or very close to it—they still do. These coastal residents were vulnerable to raids by British warships as, at the time, the American Navy was tiny compared to Britain's, whose fleet was the largest in the world.

The combination of Maine's excellent timber and its many harbors tucked into that rugged seacoast meant that Maine produced many ships. And Maine men sailed those ships to fishing grounds near and far, and traded with Europe, the Caribbean, even China. In short, Maine folks knew a thing or two about building and sailing ships—handy talents during a war.

Many Maine-built, Maine-crewed ships became privateers during the struggle for independence. These were privately owned and operated warships. Their captains held "letters of marque"—official permission from Congress to attack and seize British ships. It was a Maine privateer that brutally retaliated against the little town of Goose River, and this incident produced the ghost.

It seems that Capt. Samuel Tucker's privateer came upon a rich prize—a British merchantman heading for the British-occupied port of New York. She was carrying luxury goods for the officers and men stationed there, including tea, wine, rum, whiskey, and ale, all to boost the spirits of His Majesty's army. This ship also carried the payroll for the British army, in gold and silver coin.

It was a great day for the Americans when this rich cargo was captured by a privateer. It was a sad day for the British—all that money! All the booze! The British were furious and decided to demonstrate their anger by punishing the whole town of Goose River.

A local sailor named William Richardson, familiar with local waters, had guided Captain Tucker's prize into the tricky channels of Goose River to hide the ship and its cargo from the enemy. The local residents gladly pitched in to help hide the tea and alcohol. Then a British warship showed up. The defenseless little town was pillaged and burned by the Redcoats. How did the British know to come to Goose River? Not all Americans were supporters of the Revolution. Some, known as Tories, remained loyal to the King. It was local Tories who found out about the hidden ship and its cargo and told the British.

William Richardson knew where the ale, whiskey, rum, and wine were buried, and so as the town was rebuilt, there was plenty of drink with which to toast each American victory. The conclusion of the war was celebrated in grand style at Goose River. Richardson brought out the last of the stolen booze and urged everyone to drink up. Unfortunately, Bill mistakenly invited three Tories to join them in a toast to General Washington. They lured him to a quiet spot by the Goose River Bridge and murdered him. These Tory traitors later were caught and hanged.

And the ghost of Bill Richardson still frequents the bridge late at night, a staggering, happy drunk who will invite you to join him in a toast. Raise your tankard to General Washington and American independence! And if you are a Tory, stay clear of the bridge at Goose River.

How Hockamock Head Got Its Name

Hockamock Head is a large craggy headland or promontory on the sea passage between Bath and Boothbay Harbor. It got its name from an incident in Colonial times, when Indians attacked a small coastal settlement of Europeans. The ancient Indian nation, comprised of some twenty tribes that once occupied the land of Maine, called themselves the Abnaki or Wabanaki, "the people of the dawn." Among their beliefs, as understood by the European invaders, was that there was an evil spirit, Hockamock, whose name could be translated as "the devil."

Apparently during an Indian attack on a European village, the settlers were fleeing from the Indians. They raced away for good reason, as the Indians intended to scalp them. Now scalping is a brutal habit that seems to have been introduced to the Indians by Europeans, oddly enough.

The threat of being scalped lent a certain urgency to the fleeing Europeans. Motivation is everything. Most of the Europeans ran fast enough not to get caught before they reached the safety of their stockade. One fat, middle-aged Scotsman, wearing an old-fashioned full wig, wasn't quite fast enough. A pursuing Indian reached out, scalping knife in hand, and grabbed an apparent full head of hair. The astonished Indian ended up with a large wig in hand, while his intended victim escaped. It seemed to the Indian that he had been chasing a devil, as the seemingly headless body kept on running. The wig was dropped in superstitious horror, and the Indian cried out to his comrades, "Hockamock! Hockamock!"—"The devil! The devil!"

The Cursed Tombstone

The town of Bucksport, at the mouth of the Penobscot River, was named after its founder and leading citizen, Col. Jonathan Buck. The colonel is buried in Buck Cemetery, located near the Verona Bridge. His tombstone is an impressive towering obelisk of polished granite. On the face of this grave marker is the image of a leg and a foot. Skeptics say this is just a defect in the stone. Most townspeople call it the witch's curse.

The legend is that Jonathan Buck grew up in Haverhill, Massachusetts. There, he worked hard, prospered, and became an important enough local citizen that he was named a town judge. A beautiful young woman was brought before the judge, accused of killing a neighbor through witchcraft. There was no sign of violence on the corpse; the cause of death was unknown. However, the alleged witch had, in front of witnesses, argued with the deceased and threatened her.

Despite a distinct lack of evidence, Judge Buck found her guilty, and sentenced her to be burned at the stake. There are two versions of what happened next. One is that the accused, one Ann Harraway, told the judge that she was innocent and that her spirit someday would stand on the judge's grave and testify to the devil that Jonathan Buck knowingly had burned an innocent woman.

In the second version of the story, Ann and Jonathan were well-acquainted, so much so that Ann had borne Jonathan's illegitimate child, a son. Allegedly, this son became deranged at the sight of his mother being burned to death by judgment of his father. The son rushed into the flames and pulled out a charred leg and foot, with which he attacked Judge Buck, cursing him for his decision.

Shortly following the execution, Jonathan resigned his judgeship and went to Maine to start a new life. He founded Bucksport and lived a commendable life. When he died, in 1795, at the age of 72, his family placed a simple headstone on his grave. Soon, the headstone was defaced by the image of a leg and foot. A splendid granite shaft was commissioned to replace the first headstone. They say after it was installed, the likeness of a leg and foot appeared on it. No amount of scrubbing and sanding could remove the stain.

Is Colonel Buck's monument cursed, or is it just an accidental flaw in the stone? The monument is still there. Look and decide for yourself.

Keeping the Ghost Happy

There are many tales of pirate treasure along the Maine coast. Over the years, many have dreamed of finding such a treasure. However, such a discovery might bring with it the curse of the dead pirate.

Pirate treasure traditionally is guarded by a supernatural defense, intended to terrify anyone who might stumble across a buried chest left by buccaneers. After the treasure has been deposited in a deep hole, a crew member, or sometimes a captive sailor kidnapped from a merchant ship, would be killed on the spot. Their corpse would be laid across the chest of loot, then the hole filled in. The ghost of the dead man is charged with protecting the treasure. Should this ghost be reluctant to carry out its assigned mission, the threat is that the devil himself, a great friend of bloodthirsty pirates, will devise especially horrific tortures for the ghost down in hell.

There are those who believe, though, that a successful treasure seeker can placate the guardian ghost by giving the bones a proper burial in combination with a kind of perpetual care. The grave of the dead treasure guard must be kept neatly tended, with fresh flowers. Most importantly, the grave must receive a daily tot of rum, dribbled out on the headstone. A few drops of blood from a freshly slaughtered animal or fowl is another way to appease the spirit of the dead brigand.

There once was a farmer and fisherman on Matinous Island by name of John Wilson. Wilson was a poor man, as he was not an overly ambitious soul. He would get out of bed long after his neighbors were hard at work. He seemed to move in slow motion.

Then one day he left the island on "a business trip," he said, to distant Boston. He returned in a fine new sloop and paid cash for the best farm on the island. He built a splendid house and furnished it handsomely. Wilson married, produced a large family, and became a community leader.

An unusual feature of his new estate was a single grave behind his house. The headstone displayed no name, only the death's-head design once common on such stones. John never talked about who was buried there, but the grave always was well-tended. Oddly, a distinct odor of rum seemed to cling to the headstone.

In advanced old age, John Wilson revealed his secret. Long ago, while out duck hunting, he accidentally fell into a collapsed hole in the turf. He found himself standing in a gully in which lay an iron pot filled with Spanish gold coins. Atop this hole was a skeleton. Wilson knew enough pirate lore to carefully rebury the cursed bones after he returned from selling the gold in Boston. He honored his pact with the pirate ghost with his daily offering of rum and occasional tributes of blood. As long as the ghost of the pirate guard was appeased with honored treatment, Wilson and his family prospered.

But on John's death, despite his instructions to his children, the mysterious grave was dishonored. Overgrown with weeds, it no longer received its tributes of rum, blood, or flowers. Bad luck pursued the Wilson family, who eventually abandoned the homestead and moved off-island. It's best to keep your pact with a ghost.

Don't Deceive the Dead

Honesty is always the best policy, especially in dealing with ghosts. Many years ago, the story goes, a crew of local men from Boothbay Harbor learned that the spirit of a dead man, whose last wishes were not honored, could be an angry spirit indeed.

Squirrel Island, near Boothbay Harbor, is the site of one of the oldest settlements in Maine. It is now primarily a summer resort. Once, all of Squirrel Island was owned by Squire Greenleaf. He loved his island and knew every inch of it. The time came, in his old age, when the isolation of his beloved island was a problem for an old and infirm man. Reluctantly, he sold Squirrel Island and went to live on the mainland, at Boothbay Harbor.

Squire Greenleaf's love for Squirrel Island, and his strong bond with its many places of natural beauty, led to a rather strange request of his heirs—that his grave in Boothbay Harbor's cemetery be filled with sand from Davenport Cove, an inlet on Squirrel Island's shoreline. In life, Davenport Cove had been the Squire's most favorite place, and he wanted his body to be surrounded by its sands for eternity.

Following the death of Squire Greenleaf, a crew of men was sent in a scow to Squirrel Island to bring back sand from Davenport Cove. On the way over, the men decided that as long as the sand came from Squirrel Island, it would meet the requirements; they need not go all the way to Davenport Cove. They accordingly landed at a more convenient spot than Davenport Cove and loaded the scow with beach sand.

But when they started back to Boothbay Harbor, a terrible storm arose. The sea was churned to foam, and the cold wind howled. The scow was in danger of being swamped. Then, the crew saw a shadowy figure, resembling Squire Greenleaf, striding across the waves and gesturing angrily that they should turn back. Turn back they did, shoveling all their load of sand overboard. When the last grains of sand had gone into the sea, the storm abated as quickly as it had sprung up.

This time, they went to Davenport Cove for their load of sand, and returned to Boothbay Harbor in clear weather and calm seas. Squire Greenleaf was duly buried in genuine Davenport Cove sand, where he has rested peacefully ever since. Don't try to fool the dead.

Marie Antoinette's Ghost

In North Edgecombe, near Boothbay Harbor, sits a building known as the Marie Antoinette House. The house, high on a riverbank near the center of the little town, dates to 1774. It was originally built on Squam Island by a local sea captain, and later moved to North Edgecombe by the captain's daughter. The daughter married Samuel Clough, captain of a merchantman that carried trade between Maine and France, which is how the home became known as the Marie Antoinette House.

As unlikely as it might seem, the house is said to harbor the ghost of the tragic queen of France. The phantom appears in all the embroidered satin finery of the French court and an elaborate, towering headress bedecked with glittering jewels. Large, matched diamonds sparkle in the fabulous necklace around the apparition's neck. With haughty self-confidence, the glamorous ghost gracefully acknowledges the presence of a mere moral, and a peasant mortal at that.

This is the critical moment, according to those who have encountered the spirit of the queen. Ghostly etiquette requires the human intruder to bow deeply while backing away from the spectral royal presence. If this is done, the ghost will have disappeared when the witness lifts his or her gaze from the floor. Failure to show proper

respect for the royal ghost, however, will produce a royal tantrum. An unladylike stream of French curses will issue from the ghost, its red eyes now flashing. This is a good time to retreat. Since the ghost has never been seen outside the house, she is easy to avoid—don't go in the house, especially alone, at night.

But why would Marie Antoinette's ghost haunt a house on the coast of Maine—a state, indeed a continent, she had never visited in her life?

Marie Antoinette was born in 1755, the fourth daughter of Austrian Emperor Francis I and his queen, Maria Theresa. When she was fifteen, she married the sixteen-year-old heir of the French throne.

When Marie Antoinette and the King were imprisoned by bloodthirsty Revolutionaries, there were many plots to rescue them and smuggle them out of France. Here is where the Maine connection came in. North Edgecombe's Captain Clough conspired to rescue the queen from prison after her husband had been beheaded. His ship, the *Sally* would take her to a new life in Maine. Supposedly, many of Marie Antoinette's personal possessions—clothing, jewelry, furniture, and the like were loaded aboard *Sally.* Captain Clough wrote to his wife, telling her to expect a houseguest—the queen of France. Mrs. Clough is said to have begun a world-class house cleaning effort.

But the rescue attempt failed, and *Sally* sailed without the queen. Marie Antoinette was guillotined on August 2, 1793. Her spirit could not rest among the hateful, murderous French, and so, the story goes, her ghost sought the refuge in Maine promised her but never kept in life.

Remember to bow before her ghost, if you encounter it. Or else.

Castine's French Indian Ghost

Among the several ghosts reported to haunt the old town of Castine on Penobscot Bay is that of the town's namesake, Jean-Vincent d'Abbadie, Baron of St. Castin. This aristocrat, who usually went by the name of Castin, was born in France but spent most of his life in North America.

At the age of 15, Castin arrived in Quebec to seek his fortune in the new world. He had been given a royal grant of land at the mouth of the Penobscot River on the coast of Maine. It was a long way from Quebec City to the coast, so Castin decided on a more or less direct route overland from the St. Lawrence Valley to the Penobscot River's headwaters, where he would canoe all the way down the Penobscot. He took three Indians with him. By the time this foursome had traveled all the way to the coast of Maine, they had become good friends. Young Castin much admired his Indian companions' ability to canoe through rapids and whitewater, hunting and fishing for provisions, and navigating by the stars. He decided go "go native"—dressing and acting like an Indian. On reaching his royal grant, he made friends with the local Indians and even married the chief's daughter.

While Castin was enthusiastically taking to Indian ways, his government decided on a policy of enlisting Indian allies in their fight with the British over the destiny of North America. The series of conflicts known as the French and Indian War was about to begin. And Castin would have a starring role.

For more than thirty years, Castin fought to protect French interests and, coincidentally, his own land claims, against the English. He also fought off French pirates and Dutch attackers. The Indian alliance, in which Castin had played a central role, enabled the French to hold off the English forces using only a handful of French soldiers.

In 1688, the English successfully attacked Castin's stronghold at the settlement since named after him. Castin's own house was burned. French forces withdrew, and France never again controlled Maine.

The Baron de Castin was ordered back to France in 1701 and died there in 1717. His ghost chose to haunt Castine, Maine, the site of his greater triumphs as well as his defeat. His is an interesting ghost—a light-skinned, blue-eyed Frenchman dressed as a Penobscot Indian, from the eagle feather in his headband to his beaded deerskin and moccasins.

The Pirates of Pemaquid

Pemaquid is the site of the oldest European settlement in Maine, dating to 1625. It also is the site of ghostly visitations by the spirit of one of Maine's most famous pirates, Dixey Bull. Dixey was the most feared of pirates, and no one is completely sure that he was ever captured. He was once known as an absolutely ruthless cutthroat, but ironically, he entered the life of an outlaw only out of a righteous desire for justice. He never found the justice he sought. Some say his ghost still haunts the remains of the old fort of Pemaquid, seething with hatred for the French, the British, and the colonial Americans. The ghost of the man who lived for violence has chosen to haunt a place that witnessed a great deal of violence during its long history.

Pemaquid was the name of the Indian settlement on the site, which was documented by European explorers as early as 1569. It is located on the end of a long peninsula jutting out into the sea, and long was viewed as a strategic point. Pemaquid has a history of repeated, ultimately unsuccessful attempts to protect the settlement against invaders. No less than four forts were built on or near the site, each in turn destroyed by war.

The ghost of the notorious Dixey Bull must feel right at home in a place where the defenders always lost. Dixey started out as a peaceful, honest trader who owned his own trading sloop, *Fortune*. Dixey had the bad luck to have sailed *Fortune* into the old Plymouth Company's trading post at Castin. French forces descended on the English trading post and captured Bull's sloop with its valuable cargo. The French commander forced Dixey to write out a bill of sale for his ship and his trade goods, as though they had taken possession legally. Dixey had no choice but to comply with the charge. And that proved to be his undoing.

As a result of a temporary truce, the British canceled Bull's privateering licence against the French. Peace was official, and, according to the British government Dixey had no legal claim against the French, as they had a bill of sale to prove they'd paid for his ship and cargo. Dixey was mad enough to chew cannonballs and spit bullets. He decided to attack both French and British ships, turning pirate and giving no quarter. Both the British and the French dispatched naval vessels to find him and end his pirate career. Supposedly, he was tried and hanged for piracy in London, but many doubt this.

Many swear that Dixey Bull still prowls the streets of Pemaquid. And he's still mad at the British, the French, and just about everyone else. Can you truly blame him?

Did a UFO Buzz the Goodspeed?

Although unidentified flying objects became famous through a rash of sightings in the late 1940s, UFOs may have been seen much earlier. When reviewing some old stories about mysterious experiences, the possibility of long-ago UFO encounters arises.

In the early 1800s, the clipper ship *Goodspeed* was making her way along the Maine coast on a voyage from Halifax to Portland. It was a calm, starry night with a northeast wind filling her sails and guaranteeing a speedy arrival in port within a day or two. The night watch was uneventful, that is, until a "very bright light, spinning like a child's top, suddenly soared over the tall masts" of *Goodspeed*. "Glowing like molten iron," the mysterious object didn't make a sound as it circled the ship. It "hovered above us like a hawk riding the air currents," reported the helmsman, then suddenly it accelerated and quickly disappeared from sight.

When the *Goodspeed*'s crew told their story to others, it was considered just another tall tale, a product of too much rum and too much imagination. Did those long-ago sailors have an encounter with what we would call a UFO? Or did they just make up a good story to earn a few free drinks in a waterfront tavern?

The Pact of the Twin Sisters

At the dawn of the twentieth century, twin sisters were born to a family up in Belfast. Lucille and Linda, as they were named, were identical in every way. They developed that special, almost mystical bond so often observed between twins. They did everything together, always traveled about together, and seemed to think alike as well.

In due course, they each married and raised families of their own, still seeing one another on a frequent schedule. As they approached old age, the question arose: Would they die at the same time and make that final journey to the next world hand-in-hand as they had done so often in life?

Linda and Lucille made a secret pact together. Whichever one died first would attempt to contact the other to describe their experiences in moving to the spirit world. They agreed to a secret word to be included in any message from the spirit world in order to prove

that a message was genuine and not a fraudulent one from a fake spiritualist. The secret word was "sapphire," their favorite gem.

Lucille died first. Mourning her loss, Linda waited anxiously for some contact from her dead twin. But no message from beyond arrived.

About a year after Lucille's death, however, Linda summoned her family to her home. She asked them to stay with her that evening, as her twin had, at last, made contact from beyond the grave. Lucille had appeared to her early that morning. Her phantom had walked through a closed door and moved about the room as though she were swimming in the air rather than walking. "Sapphire, my dear sister, sapphire," she said. "You will join me this night between midnight and one o'clock. Do not fear but have faith that you will join me in a wonderful new plane of existence."

Linda's family tried to reassure her that she had just had a bad dream. When Linda could not be dissuaded that she was about to die, they offered to call a doctor to stand by if she had a heart attack or some other misfortune. "No" replied Linda, "I know that I'll soon rejoin my sister. I'm not afraid." Soon after her clock struck twelve, Linda fell into a deep coma and passed away quickly within the hour. Just as Lucille had predicted, the twins were together once more.

The Ghost Who Likes Pets

A family moving into an old house in the little fishing port of Rockland had a most unusual encounter with a ghost. The ghost of a previous occupant of their house apparently liked dogs and cats so much that it likes to hold open house for stray dogs and cats in the neighborhood. This hospitable ghost is continuing a habit, formed in her lifetime, of feeding any cats or dogs that happen by her house. Of course, it isn't the ghost's house anymore—or is it? The present inhabitants of the house must wonder just whose house it is as they find themselves the somewhat unwilling hosts of furry visitors.

It started innocently enough. The family had just moved in and were unpacking. A large, rather weathered-looking earthenware bowl had been left by the now-deceased previous occupant. It was found by the steps to the back porch, evidently having been used to hold water for a pet dog or cat. The new owners ignored the bowl as they moved in. It was a few days after moving day when the husband noticed that the bowl was always filled with fresh water. He had assumed that his wife had kept it refilled for the occasional stray dog or cat that might be thirsty. However, when he questioned whether they should be encouraging strays, the wife denied filling the bowl. That was a puzzle: Who was keeping the bowl filled for the refreshment of dogs and cats in the neighborhood?

The puzzle grew. Sometimes a saucer of milk appeared beside the water bowl, to the delight of cats. The milk, it turned out, was coming from the household supply, but who was putting if there? Then, leftover meat, fish, or chicken tidbits from their refrigerator began to make their way to the bowl by the steps, only to be swiftly consumed by whatever animal happened to stop by. "We're running a restaurant for dogs and cats!" said the wife, "and we didn't plan to!"

On questioning their neighbors, the couple learned that old Mrs. Meeks, a lonely widow who had lived in the house for many years before them, had been in the habit of feeding stray animals. The house's new owners concluded that the ghost of Mrs. Meeks was still looking after her hungry, temporary "guests," although they never actually saw the hospitable ghost. They decided that they would not even try to interfere with such a kind-hearted ghost. After all, some ghosts are much more of a problem than a ghost who feeds strays!

The Phantom Fiery Infant

Be forewarned. The story of this ghost's origins is very disturbing. A brutal incident produced a terrifying apparition—a ghostly image that, according to the story, reappears on the occasions of a family member's death—a family that still struggles under the curse of a foul deed committed long ago by a truly evil ancestor.

Late one night, frantic knocking at her door awakened the town midwife. Her services were required most urgently, reported her midnight caller, a coachman driving an elegant coach. There was one unusual stipulation—the birth was to occur in secret, and the midwife had to agree to be blindfolded before being taken to her patient in the private coach. A generous handful of gold coins convinced her to cooperate.

When her blindfold at last was removed, the midwife found herself looking at a lovely young woman in labor. She did not wear a wedding ring. Soon, an infant boy was delivered. The child appeared to be having trouble breathing. "We must get a doctor," advised the midwife "No!" was the stern reply of an older, elegantly dressed gentleman the midwife had not noticed previously. "I won't have this scandal known—it would ruin my reputation," declared the man, obviously the infant's father but not married to the mother.

After an agonizing few minutes, the poor child breathed its last. "This child must have a Christian burial," sobbed the young mother. "I'll not stand for any public disgrace!" thundered the father, who seized the tiny corpse and threw it into the burning fireplace. To the horror of both midwife and mother, the infant soon was consumed by the flames.

Badly shaken, the midwife allowed herself to be again blindfolded for her return home. "Not a word to anyone," warned the man. "I'm a powerful man in this town, and I'll destroy you if you talk. Every month, you'll get a purse of money as long as this remains secret." Within days, the midwife committed suicide, but not before telling her tale.

The legend is that the illustrious family of which the ill-fated infant's father was a member has lived with a curse ever since. When the man who had consigned his dead illegitimate son to the flames faced his own death, the image of a fiery infant appeared before him. Confronted by the terrifying reminder of his own evil, the man died screaming, his face a mask of pure terror. And, ever since, the fiery infant's ghost appears to foretell the death of a member of this family. How many generations will face the specter of the fiery infant? No one knows. There is no one to ask.

The Watcher of Monhegan Island

This ghost is seldom seen, but those who've encountered her will never forget her. There is a weird legend on Monhegan Island about the phantom known as the Watcher.

The story is that a wealthy older businessman visited Monhegan in the 1880s to recuperate from a long illness. He got into the habit of taking long, solitary walks along the rocky shoreline. One day in early autumn, he strolled out on a lonely little peninsula, enjoying the brisk sea air. As he was staring out to sea, he became aware of another figure standing near him, also looking out over the waves.

It was a lovely young woman, wrapped in a flowing dark cloak. Her long blond hair framed a pale, oval face with large, melancholy blue eyes. She appeared to be so preoccupied that she ignored the man until he ventured a polite greeting. She turned abruptly to stare at him and then said, "He will come again," emphasizing the "will." With that she turned and walked away, disappearing behind a boulder.

The gentleman did not mention this brief event back at his boardinghouse that evening but he decided to return to that same locale the next day. Intrigued by her beauty as much as by her cryptic comment, he looked forward to seeing her again. Sure enough, she reappeared at the same isolated spot the next day. And, once again, her only words were, "He will come again."

This time the man observed that, despite a persistent wind, the woman's long hair lay undisturbed. Her cloak never rustled, its folds absolutely straight even as she walked. Most oddly, the stiff, dry grass and delicate seashells over which she walked remained unmarked by her passage. Was she a wraithlike spirit rather than a living human? And who was this mysterious man who would come again?

That evening, the gentleman mentioned his odd experience to an oldtimer of his acquaintance, a retired fisherman. He also admitted to having seen the Watcher, as he called her. "She is a ghost," said the longtime Monhegan resident, "and she has a mission to guard the treasure." The story was that 100 years before, bold pirates had cruised these waters, pillaging settlements on land and capturing ships at sea. Among them was the notorious Captain Teach, also known as Blackbeard. One of Blackbeard's comrades, a Captain Scott, brought the lovely lady with him when he landed on Monhegan to bury treasure. She stayed behind on the island to guard the treasure and await his return, whereupon they were to wed.

But on his next voyage of plundering and mayhem, Captain Scott and all his crew vanished when their ship's ample powder magazine blew up, splintering the ship and shredding the crew.

And so, the lady still watches for her captain, still faithfully guarding his immense, ill-gotten treasure, watching for a reunion that will never happen, at least on this earth.

Laying the Library Ghost to Rest

A common theory about ghosts is that they have remained in this world after death only because they have not yet completed some task or mission. Once their goal has been achieved, their spirit can truly rest in peace and move on to the next plane of existence. Such was the case of the library ghost of Bar Harbor.

This ghost haunted the library of one of Bar Harbor's elegant seaside "cottages," huge mansions occupied only seasonally by their wealthy owners. This was a particularly persistent ghost, finally laid to rest through the actions of a family friend and amateur ghost hunter.

The ghost appeared only in the library. According to family legend, this phantom took the shape of an old man, dressed formally in the style of the Victorian era. The ghost would appear to anyone who happened to be in the library around midnight, frequently leaning over the shoulder of a midnight reader. The spirit seemed to be particularly interested in an old rolltop desk in the library, said to have been owned by the founder of the family fortune. When any family members encountered this spirit, they fled in panic. When a family friend expressed interest in meeting this ghost, the present owners of the house quickly agreed.

The self-proclaimed ghost hunter settled in for a long evening. But despite his staying in the library well past midnight, no apparition presented itself. The family members expressed disappointment, but the ghost hunter advised patience and visited the library again late at night.

This time, patience was rewarded. The smokelike image of an old gentleman made his appearance at the elbow of his human visitor. When the intrepid ghost hunter did not bolt from the room but remained calm, the ghost drifted toward the old desk. "Papers," whispered the ghost, "papers must be burned," indicating a closed desk drawer. The family friend found a dusty bundle of documents hidden under an old business accounting book. While the ghostly image of the old man hovered anxiously by his side, the ghost hunter scanned the documents.

Finally, the cause of the ghost's anxiety and persistence became clear. The old papers revealed an embarrassing family secret—the prestigious, socially prominent family's fortune had originated in a smuggling operation many years before.

The ghost was the founder of the operation, a smuggler who was ashamed of the illegal foundations of his fortune and reputation. "Papers must be burned," again insisted the ghost. The family friend threw the incriminating papers into the fireplace. The ghost disappeared, never to return. Mission accomplished, by both ghost and ghost hunter.

The Curse of Captain Kidd's Gold

The infamous pirate, Captain Kidd, is known to have frequented the coast of Maine. Like other pirates of his day, William Kidd is supposed to have buried treasure chests at secret locations along the coast, planning to retrieve the treasure at a later date.

If Captain Kidd, who was hanged for piracy in London in 1701, buried as many treasure chests on the East Coast of America as legends claim, he would have been too busy digging holes to go out and capture merchant ships. Over the centuries, hundreds, perhaps thousands of treasure seekers have excavated alleged treasure sites from Nova Scotia to Virginia and the Carolinas. There is no proof that anyone ever found Kidd's treasure hoard, but not for want of trying.

There is a persistent rumor that one of America's greatest fortunes can be traced back to Captain Kidd. Since Kidd's stock of gold, silver, and jewels was the product of a ruthless criminal enterprise, the fortune founded on the pirate's loot is said to be cursed and, furthermore, cursed into the third generation.

A century after Kidd's death on the gallows, his treasure is said to have been found on Deer Isle, near the mouth of the Penobscot River. The legend, which has always been stoutly denied by his family, is that John Jacob Astor and an associate found the treasure. Astor was a fur trader who traded with Indians in Maine and spent some time in the area. No doubt he was a shrewd trader, but his fortunes seemed to grow, literally, overnight. Was it just luck, or had he found pirate gold and jewels? Supposedly, in 1801, Astor's Manhattan bank account suddenly went from $4,000 to over $500,000. A London dealer in precious stones sent him checks over two years totaling $1,350,000. Just how many beaver pelts did that represent?

Fortunately for his son and grandson, John Jacob the first invested heavily in Manhattan real estate. His grandson, Col. John Jacob Astor III, was worth about $150 million when he met his tragic death. He owned 700 lots in Manhattan alone. A Harvard graduate, he was a keenly intelligent man who patented several inventions and even wrote a novel. He was most accomplished and fortunate —until his luck ran out on the night of April 14, 1912, when he went down with the *Titanic.*

Was he the victim of the curse of Captain Kidd's treasure, visited on the grandson of the man who found it, or was it just plain bad luck?

Lost in Time and Space

Many stories of supernatural sightings involve what some call "time slips," that is, a person or an object appears in the wrong time or place. In these cases, a real person, or even a whole army, or a movable object like a vehicle or ship, appears in a place or time context different from their actual life or history.

When someone or something appears in an unlikely time and space convergence, it appears in ghostly form. Why do persons or objects return as spiritual images or phantoms? Are they revisiting a place and time that had special importance to them during their lifetime? Interestingly, these apparitions, lost in time and space, seldom threaten or even try to frighten the living.

Many seamen and fishermen have seen a phantom ship sailing before the wind in the ocean off the shipbuilding center of Bath. The ghost ship is described as a clipper ship, of the design made famous around the world when American clippers set speed records.

Maine has long been an important shipbuilding center. The state's forests were the prime reason for this long-standing preeminence in the age of wooden ships. The first ship built in North America by Englishmen, the *Virginia,* was launched from the banks of the Kennebek River in 1608. For many years, Maine built more ships than any other state. In the years just before the Civil War, Maine supplied more than half of all American tonnage.

Maine didn't just lead in quantity, it had a reputation for quality as well, building the best sailing ships in the world. A triumph of Maine shipbuilding was the famed clipper ship *Red Jacket,* launched in 1854. *Red Jacket* once crossed the Atlantic from New York to England in exactly thirteen days, one hour and twenty-five minutes, setting a record that still stands.

The clipper had a distinct profile—a sleek, narrow hull with four, sometimes five, towering masts carrying many sails to propel the ships with speeds not seen again until the age of steam. The phantom clipper off the coasts of Maine is thought to be *Red Jacket*, reliving her moment of glory. *Red Jacket*'s materialization seems to follow a pattern, as described by sailors who've seen her. It happens on calm evenings with no wind and glassy seas. Suddenly, the ghostly clipper appears following the observer's ships and quickly closing the distance separating them. The startled crew of the modern ship report that the mysterious sailing ship does not show on radar. Electronically, the clipper ship does not exist. She flies by, easily outracing the other ship, her sails billowing despite a lack of wind. No hand steadies her great wheel; no sailors are visible on deck or in her rigging. Her flag snaps in an invisible breeze. The clipper speeds out of sight, leaving behind only an amazed and puzzled crew. Most observers swear that the phantom ship leaves no wake as she speeds on toward England, reliving her triumph of long ago.

Down East

THIS LARGE EXTENT OF RUGGED COAST IN THE NORTH GOES FROM WINTER Harbor, across Frenchman's Bay from Bar Harbor, to the Canadian border at Eastport, which is just across the channel from President Franklin Roosevelt's summer home in Campobello, New Brunswick.

The Phantom Pirate Ship

Most have heard about the legend of the "Flying Dutchman"—a ghost ship that sails on and on, and will never reach port, its sailors' spirits cursed to never see land again. The coastal waters of Maine boast many such phantom ships. Machiasport was home to one such cursed vessel, the pirate ship *Whidaw*.

One reason why piracy seemed to be so common in the waters off the American colonies in the century before the Revolution was the phenomenon of privateering. Privateers were privately owned ships that had official permission, and encouragement, to attack and capture trading ships sailing under an enemy's flag. A legal document known as letters of marque gave the captain powers to detain, seize, and take enemy vessels, and bring them into port for legal prosecution under the powers of war.

One factor that encouraged piracy was the ease with which looted cargoes could be sold. The British mercantile acts, which forbade American colonists to trade directly with anyone but England, were quite unpopular in the colonies. It was almost an act of patriotism to buy smuggled goods or items of unknown origin from shady characters who assured their customers that the goods had "fallen off the wagon."

In the early eighteenth century, a pirate named Samuel Bellamy actually built a fortified base for his pirate voyages. His fort was on the Machias River near present-day Machiasport. He left his fort only when in search of, as he said himself, "loot, recruits, and women," not necessarily in that order.

Sam saw himself as a kind of seagoing Robin Hood. Whenever he captured a ship, he would try to persuade its crew to join him. He argued that all men had as much right as the owners and captains who, armed with their letters of marque, stole and got away with it. He had a point, and many sailors saw it and joined.

On his fateful last voyage, Sam was plundering ships off the coast of Nova Scotia when he mistakenly attacked a French warship. He came close to losing that fight; his ship, the *Whidaw* was damaged seriously, which made it difficult to maneuver. Sailing south, he captured a whaler out of New Bedford. Her captain pretended to join forces with Samuel Bellamy but treacherously led the *Whidaw* toward a sand bank. The whaler turned away from danger at the last moment. The crippled *Whidaw,* however, could not respond fast enough to the change in direction and wrecked. Bellamy and his crew all drowned as *Whidaw* sank.

Though *Whidaw*'s wooden bones lie on the bottom of the sea among the bones of her sailors and master, there have been many sightings over the years of the ship scudding along under full sail and flying the dreaded black flag of piracy. Is the Robin Hood of the sea doomed to sail on forever, looking for another victim to loot?

Using Witchcraft Against a Witch

There are good witches, and there are bad witches. Some witches use their knowledge of spells, potions, and incantations to help people, while others use their secret powers for evil. Especially evil are those witches who, like old Mrs. Hicks who once lived in Jonesport, used the threat of witchcraft to extort things from their neighbors. They tell a good story about how a nice Christian lady managed to turn witchcraft back on the notorious witch, Mrs. Hicks. Of course, whether you believe this story depends on how you feel about witches and witchcraft. There is an old saying in Maine that,

Where folks believe in witches, witches are:
But where they don't believe, there ain't no witches thar.

A lot of Maine folks believe, so witches must be there. Among the believers was Peggy Beal. A fine churchgoing lady, Peggy didn't want to believe in witches. But an acquaintance living in Jonesport, a short ferry ride from Beals Island where Peggy lived, seemed to possess supernatural powers. Mrs. Hicks, it seems, always wanted to "borrow" something from Peggy, and these borrowed items never were returned. If Peggy refused to loan the item sought by Mrs. Hicks, it disappeared. Old Mrs. Hicks always made her requests for a loan in person; if refused, she would stare at her victim with the "evil eye," striking fear in those who refused her. She didn't experience many refusals.

One day, Mrs. Hicks demanded of Peggy the loan of a whole sheep. Peggy was not poor, but a whole sheep? This was just too much. "No!" was the answer. Sure enough, the next day the sheep was found dead of no apparent cause.

A sailor from Salem, where everyone believed in witchcraft, and for good reason, gave Peggy some sage advice. "Build a hot fire," he directed, "and scorch the wool all over the sheep while reciting your favorite passage from the Bible. Then, Mrs. Hicks will thrice demand something of you. You must refuse each time, offering instead to lend her your Bible."

Peggy followed his instructions exactly. One day later came the news that old Mrs. Hicks was dead. Folks on Beals Island still pat the gravestone of Peggy Beal, just for luck, in case there really is such a thing as witches.

Do you believe? Then they really are there.

The Legend of Tom Cook

About two centuries ago, a local boy in Calais became a legend in his own time. Tom Cook became known as the "leveler," because his actions "leveled out" the differences between rich and poor. Tom was Maine's version of Robin Hood. The devil made him do it, in a way.

It was way back before the American Revolution. Little Tom lay sick, very sick. His parents feared that he was dying. The doctor had tried everything, but Tom kept getting weaker, his little body consumed by fever. As was the custom of the day, the local parson was called in to pray over him. He offered fervent prayers, concluding with, "Let the Lord's will be done." "No!" exclaimed his mother, "spare his life. I care not about the Lord's will—I want my child to live!" Blasphemy, true, but a heartfelt plea, and little Tom recovered. Had his mother made a pact with the devil by her agonized rejection of God's will?

Tom Cook grew up so full of mischief that people thought he must have become a servant of the evil one. And in truth, his soul was claimed by the devil, who showed up one day to drag his disciple into hell. But Tom was possessed of a quick wit, and was not fundamentally bad—just a lively boy with disdain for the rules of society. Maybe God hadn't altogether given up on Tom. When the devil told Tom he had come for him, Tom asked for a moment to first put on his galluses (suspenders). "You don't want to drag me out with my pants falling down!" The devil, who considered himself a gentleman, agreed to the last request. Tom promptly threw his galluses into a fire, and therefore could never put them on, so he could not be forced to answer the devil's summons. Outsmarted, the devil withdrew to pout down in hell.

Tom, safe now from the devil, embarked on a career of crime, but he considered it a good cause. He called himself a "leveler," stealing from the rich and giving to the poor. He would steal a roast turkey from a rich man's table and drop it off in the kitchen of a poor family. Children flocked around him, for he always had pockets crammed with stolen toys and candy. When a poor old neighbor lay sick on her miserable bed of straw, Tom stole a fine feather bed to comfort her. Sacks of flour would mysteriously disappear from stores, only to be deposited at the back doors of families in want.

When Tom finally was captured by the sheriff, a jury was called to judge him. Many of the jurymen had recently dined on food donated to them by Tom, so he was found not guilty. When Tom Cook the leveler died of old age, most in the community prayed that he would be judged by the good results of his bad behavior. The devil might have saved him from an early death, but Tom fed many a hungry person in his day.

The Blue Rock and the Green Flame

This unusual story is said to have happened near the little town of Jonesport. Close to this fishing village is a tiny island, more like a large rock. A sheltered cove features a little crescent of sand, and this miniature beach is dominated by a large blue rock. That blue rock was the locale of a fantastic tale told by the island's sole inhabitant, a lobsterman.

It was around the time of the Revolution. Coastal dwellers had learned to be wary of strange ships in these waters, as both patriots and British interests were being served by privateers. These privateers were ruthless and were known to switch sides quickly in the interest of seizing a rich prize. And so our solitary lobsterman was properly suspicious and careful to remain hidden when an unknown ship approached one dark night. The ship flew no flag, nor was there any name painted on her bows. Soon after the anchor was dropped, a small boat was launched, and six sturdy sailors rowed ashore. What happened next so terrified the island's only occupant that he waited until he was on his deathbed decades later to tell his story, a story that has inspired many reckless attempts to dig for treasure.

The sailors dug a deep hole by the blue rock, figuring the boulder would make a convenient and memorable landmark. A great iron pot was lowered into the hole. Then the captain of this crew stepped back from the hole as all his men doffed their caps and stood with heads bowed. The captain muttered an invocation to "Satan, the father of all pirates" and tossed a small green package into the deep hole. Instantly, there was a great blinding green flash and a loud explosion. As the smoke cleared, it could be seen that the hole had disappeared, the spot marked only by scorched earth.

But the story doesn't stop there. When the lobsterman at last told his family this astounding story, his surviving sons were determined to dig up the iron pot to see if it really contained treasure. Not wishing to share the loot, if any, they waited until a moonless night. No sooner had they begun to dig, when a great old sailing ship approached their little island from the open sea. No man stood at the helm, yet the ship was skillfully steered around rocks and ledges. No sailors appeared on the rigging, yet the sails were furled at just the right moment as the ship's keel grated onto the sand. A large plank was run out of the side of the ship as if by its own accord.

With horrible yells, a mob of skeletons swarmed off the ship onto the beach, brandishing swords and shovels. As the terrified brothers watched from behind cover, the skeletons dug a deep hole by the blue rock. Soon, a great covered iron pot was unearthed. The skeletons opened the lid, revealing a glistening pile of gold coins. Taking a few handfuls of coins, the gruesome crew of skeletons then covered the pot. A green flame leaped skyward with a deafening roar, and the hole was filled in an instant. The ship sailed away as silently and mysteriously as it had come, leaving behind only a scorched patch of rocky soil next to the blue rock. And, of course, two badly frightened men.

Others have been tempted to dig up the pot of gold, but when they begin to dig, an unmanned ship appears, silently gliding toward the beach. The would-be treasure hunters flee for their lives. Wouldn't you?

The Ghosts of the Harbor Boys

The tiny town of Winter Harbor, across Frenchmen's Bay from better-known Bar Harbor, is the scene of an old tale of seagoing ghosts called the Harbor Boys. Winter Harbor earned its name by the fact that, no matter how cold the winter, ice never forms on its waters, allowing ships to use it all winter long.

On dark, stormy nights, many a sailor or fisherman in the vicinity of Winter Harbor has heard the cry, "Row boys, row! Row for your lives!" above the roar of the wind. "Help!" echoes across the turbulent waters. But there is no one there at daybreak, nor is any wreckage or bodies ever found.

The terrified cries for help are said to come from the ghosts of the cutthroat gang who called themselves the Harbor Boys and once terrified many a Maine harbor during the American Revolution. The Harbor Boys were made up of army deserters from both the British and American armies. They had no loyalties except to their own greed and bloodlust, though they sometimes claimed to be loyal to King George. Even King George would have been horrified and disgusted by the actions of the Harbor Boys, though, as these desperadoes ruthlessly pillaged, raped, and burned isolated towns and villages along the Maine coast. They attacked under the cover of darkness, committing their foul deeds and fleeing before the dawn.

The Harbor Boys would navigate by using the lights on shore—candles and lanterns of houses—as their guides. They used large rowboats or galleys, usually with six or eight oarsmen and a helmsman, so that no sails or masts would alert townspeople to their sneak attack.

But somehow, the citizens of Winter Harbor learned of a planned raid on their village. The defenders hit on an idea to lure the attackers onto the rocks rather than into the safe harbor they sought. Accordingly, all lights in town that fateful night were extinguished. Instead, a few lanterns were placed on the jagged rocks that guarded the entrance to Winter Harbor.

Sure enough, the rogues' boat helmsman steered for the rocks, thinking he was aiming for the harbor. Finally alerted to danger by the sound of the surf pounding on the rocks, the helmsman changed direction shouting, "Row boys, row for your lives!"

It was too late. The thugs lost their lives, dashed upon the rocks by heavy seas. The town was saved. And on dark, stormy nights, the phantom Harbor Boys relive their final abortive assault on a helpless but clever community.

Maine's Own Paul Bunyan

Folks on Beals Island, near Jonesport, believe that the ghost of Barney Beal, "Tall Barney," can be seen occasionally on the island named for his father, Manwaring Beal, the first settler here. Tall Barney is said to have stood six feet, seven inches and was possessed of superhuman strength. His feats of strength and fearless disposition earned him fame as "the Cock of the Walk" along the coast from Quoddy Head to Cape Elizabeth. It is said that when Barney sat in a chair, his hands touched the floor. When he spoke, everyone listened.

It wasn't a good idea to mess with Tall Barney. Once, he was fishing off Grand Manan Island, which is part of the Canadian Province of New Brunswick. Some armed English sailors objected to an American catching fish in Canadian waters and tried to board Barney's boat at gunpoint. The legend is that Barney grabbed their guns and broke them over his knee. He then tossed the broken guns and terrified men back into their boat, with a suggestion that they leave him alone. They did. Another time, on a visit to Rockland, a runaway horse was dragging a beer wagon down a street, careening into bystanders. Barney knocked the horse senseless with one blow of his fist. He took a barrel of beer off the wagon as his reward and swallowed it in one draft. In a Portland saloon, a gang of sailors made the mistake of making fun of Barney's "down east" accent. He sent all fifteen of them to the hospital.

Tall Barney makes a very impressive ghost. Should you meet a six foot, seven inch spirit on Beals Island, just cross to the other side of the street while nodding hello. Nobody messes with Barney.

A Dead Hand Rocks the Cradle

Most Maine folks are, by necessity, thrifty. They don't throw away anything that might be useful. And living by the sea provides an occasional free gift in the form of flotsam.

Many years ago, up by Machiasport, a terrible winter gale was blowing. Elizabeth Skinner could have sworn that she heard a baby's cries in the midst of the storm. Her husband didn't think it was possible to hear a baby over the howling winds and pelting rain, but Elizabeth, a mother four times over, knew better. On the morning after the storm, she strolled along the beach, looking carefully for anything useful brought in by the waves. All she found was a baby's cradle—beautifully made and in fine condition. Of course, she took it home, as she had an infant at the time to put in it.

She noticed an odd thing about that cradle—it would rock during storms. "It's just the vibrations from the floorboards when the wind hits the house," said her husband, "nothing to worry about." But then her sister Harriet came to visit. Harriet had second sight—she could see things that others could not.

"Who is that woman rocking the cradle?" she asked of Elizabeth. "The cradle always rocks during a gale," was the reply. "No, a woman dressed all in black is rocking the cradle. Her face is deathly white, and there is seaweed in her hair," observed Harriet.

Elizabeth was thoroughly spooked. She took the cradle, chopped it into pieces, and made a bonfire of it. And while the cradle burned, the most unearthly screams were heard, as though a baby and its mother were in terrible pain. When the cradle was reduced to ashes, the screaming stopped. Elizabeth doesn't go beachcombing anymore.

Remember to Bring the Bible

Most ghosts seem to be very territorial. They have their haunts, literally, and stay there. Occasionally, one hears of a phantom that seems tied to a specific person or family, seemingly traveling with its living hosts wherever they might happen to go. Such was the experience of a haunted family in Eastport, the easternmost seaport in Maine.

In the late nineteenth century, this family was haunted by a particularly nasty poltergeist. What the family had done to attract the attention of this very active and very obnoxious spirit was a mystery. The poltergeist smashed an entire set of fine china as, one by one, dishes, saucers, and cups flew off the table seemingly by themselves. Once, a pot of boiling water sailed off the stove, just missing the mother. Children's toy trains and wagons careened across the floor, propelled by an unseen hand. Heavy potted plants danced across rooms to smash into walls. In short, the poltergeist was making life hell for the family. But what to do?

In desperation, the family decided to confide in their parish priest. They had not talked about their unnerving experiences with anyone outside the family, not wishing to be thought weird by their friends and neighbors.

Their priest was sympathetic. He came to the house to counsel them. He was not authorized to attempt an exorcism, he explained. But he had a suggestion. Perhaps the family could discourage the evil presence in their house by gathering every evening and reading aloud from the Bible. God's word might drive out the poltergeist, or at least keep it quiet. He made a point of blessing the family Bible before he left.

It worked. As the daily Bible reading sessions progressed, the poltergeist's appearances became less and less frequent, finally ceasing altogether. What a relief!

Decades later, the older generation had died out. The surviving son moved his family to a more up-to-date house in a new suburb. The family tradition of an evening Bible reading session was forgotten. The family Bible was even left behind in the move to the new house.

Things began to happen. A glass vase flew off a table. Pictures fell off their wall hooks. Doors opened and shut by themselves. The poltergeist, almost forgotten, had returned with a vengeance.

Frantic, the son asked permission to look through the attic of his former home. He found the family Bible and restored it to his new home. The family Bible-reading tradition was reinstituted. Again, the poltergeist's activities tapered off and ceased. Don't forget your Bible when you move.

Don't Get Lost near Eastport

"Down east" on the Maine coast folks know to beware of "north-easters"—storms whose winds blow out of the northeast. They can blow up suddenly, and in winter, drop a heavy load of snow. Joshua was a traveling pharmaceutical salesman who just recently had been assigned to a new territory in northern and eastern Maine. Unfamiliar with northeasters, Joshua was unwary enough to find himself on a lonely back road not far from the Canadian border. He'd expected to spend the night in Eastport, but the rapidity with which the roads were being covered in deep snow suggested a change of plans. He spotted a small sign advertising a bed and breakfast outside a large and rather gloomy-looking house set back from the road.

Bed and breakfast sounded good, as the alternative was trying to drive through a snowstorm on unfamiliar back roads. His knock was answered by a gaunt, older woman who seemed a little surprised to find a guest on her doorstep. Did she have a room available? Yes indeed, was the reply—he'd have his choice as he was the only guest. Joshua persuaded his hostess to provide some supper, although she usually cooked only breakfasts for guests. "I wouldn't mind eating a breakfast now," said Joshua, who soon was dining on bacon, eggs, and blueberry pancakes. After his unconventional supper, Joshua offered to share the contents of his pocket flask of whiskey. The old woman grew noticeably friendlier.

"Tell me about this house," suggested Joshua, who couldn't help noticing that the place looked like a time capsule from the nineteenth century. It had been built, she reported, by her great-grandfather, who'd made his fortune in lumber. His misfortune was to have a son who rebelled against his parent's strict moral code and showed no interest in the lumber business. To the son, the chief asset of the area was not trees, but the location near Canada, for this was during Prohibition and liquor smuggling was a thriving industry.

The son soon became a major player in the smuggling opera-tions importing liquor from Canada and sending it south to thirsty Americans. Most smugglers sampled their own wares, and the son became locally famous for his wild parties and wilder friends. His widowed father was appalled by the loud, drunken parties thrown by his son, and customarily remained in his upstairs bedroom while drunken orgies raged on the first floor. The invalid father took refuge in his religion and was prone to sermonizing when face to face with his wayward son.

The son laughed off his father's warnings of the wrath of God and often joked about his father's piety. That is what caused the tragedy, said the old woman, "What tragedy?" queried Joshua, by now on his third whiskey. "It was during a particularly drunken affair hosted by his son," recounted the old lady, "when the inebri-ated crowd decided to have some fun with the poor old man. They insisted on invading his bedroom and dragging him downstairs. There was an empty chair at the table, and he must join them for a drink, they said. But no sooner had the old man been seated when he fell forward at the table, dead," recalled his hostess as they drained the last drop of whiskey.

Joshua went up to his bedroom and soon was sound asleep. Until, that is, the cars began to arrive. The sounds of arriving cars and slamming doors awakened Joshua and sent him to the window. To his amazement, he saw a fleet of vintage cars from the 1920s—Cadillacs, Lincolns, Packards, Pierce Arrows, even a Bentley, filling the snow-covered drive. The sounds of jazz and drunken laughter drifted up from the first floor.

Suddenly, there was loud knocking at his door, which a fright-ened Joshua tried to ignore. Two burly drunks burst into the room and grabbed the unwilling salesman. They marched him downstairs, where a large gathering of men in tuxedoes and women in beaded, twenties-style gowns were tossing back cocktails.

"We have an empty chair!" they roared, "You must join us." "Won't you have a drink?" they shouted, their strangely red eyes glit-tering with evil. Absolutely terrified, Joshua remembered his Sunday school days. He stood up and began praying with all the sincerity he had, "Dear Lord, deliver me from evil," he began. Suddenly, there was a huge crash of lightning, and Joshua passed out. When he awoke in the morning, he dressed quickly and went down to find the old lady, who was placidly fixing breakfast for her only guest. "Where did everyone go?" he demanded. "Everyone?" asked the woman, "Why, you and I are alone here." "What happened to all the cars?" he said. "Cars? There are no cars other than yours, look at the snow outside—the plow hasn't done over the road yet—you'll have plenty of time for breakfast. Are bacon and eggs again alright?"

The "Dutchess" Knocks on the Door

This intriguing bit of family history only recently was shared by an elderly member of the family. For reasons that will be obvious, the family's true name will not be used. Instead, we'll call them the Wellingtons.

The Wellingtons made a fortune by setting up a knitting mill on the banks of the Machias River, where the swift current turned the water wheel that provided free energy. In the late nineteenth century, money just poured into the family coffers. The lady of the house, as the locals would say, began to "put on airs"—that is, she began to act as though she were a member of some glorified aristocracy instead of just the richest family in the small town of Machiasport.

Emily Wellington was fascinated by British royalty: to her, the epitome of class. This was the Victorian age—named for Queen Victoria, who had a huge influence on fashions of her day. Whatever Queen Victoria did, wore, or even ate or drank instantly was copied, not just in Britain but among many Americans as well. When, for example, Mrs. Wellington heard that Queen Victoria favored a particular shade of lavender for her clothes, then her wardrobe suddenly blossomed in lavender as well.

Emily was fond of being driven about town in an elegant open carriage, drawn by a pair of matched black horses. Her coachman was required to wear a top hat, English style. Emily would nod and wave graciously to friends as she made her way about town.

All of this pretension was a little wearing on folks, even among her relatives and close friends, who began referring to Emily as "the Dutchess," behind her back of course. This nickname stuck, and townspeople would openly refer to her as the Dutchess, not as a compliment.

Putting on airs, was not Emily's only annoying habit. She was a domineering person, intensely interested in everyone else's private affairs. She eavesdropped shamelessly, always wanting to know what was going on. It must have been a relief, in some ways, to her family when Emily died at a ripe old age. She was buried with appropriate pomp, with an elaborate tombstone to mark her grave.

But did she stay in her grave? Her family began to fear that she was with them still. A very large oil painting of Emily, in her best imitation of Queen Victoria's dress and jewelry, dominated the living room. Hung above the fireplace, the portrait was the centerpiece of the room. More than one family member complained that the picture's face appeared to turn slightly as people moved about the room. The portrait's glittering eyes seemed to grow larger if juicy gossip was being discussed. Was the portrait haunted?

In life, Emily had disliked being in a dark room, even while asleep. She always had a lamp or candle burning when in a room. After her death, the family members noticed that a lamp or candle near Emily's portrait would relight itself after being extinguished, as the room was emptied at bedtime. A light would burn all night in the room where Emily's image was displayed.

A family conference was held. Was Emily's ghost somehow contained within her picture? Her survivors were uneasy about using the room where Emily stared at them from within the ornate picture frame. It was decided to move the picture to the second floor hallway.

No sooner had that been done when the real trouble started. It was the custom in those days before central heating to keep interior doors in the house shut, at least during Maine winters. It reduced cold drafts that way. The family was settled comfortably in the living room, a roaring fire in the fireplace. There was a distinct knock on the living room door. But when the door was opened, there was no one there. A sudden chill enveloped the room. The fire died abruptly in the fireplace, and all the candles and oil lamps blew out. In the darkness the family members thought they heard the once familiar rustle of the silk skirts the Dutchess loved to wear.

When the lights were relit, there was no sign of a visitor, dead or alive. The next evening, the knock at the living room door went unanswered by the frightened family. Then they heard a scream from upstairs. A young child, put to bed early, had been awakened by footsteps in the hallway. On opening the door, the child was terrified to see that the portrait of the Dutchess at the top of the stairs was only a black silhouette of the lady rather than her face. Had the Dutchess left her picture to descend the stairs and knock on the door? By morning, Emily's face had returned to her portrait.

A hurried family council determined to exile the Dutchess's picture from the house. They feared to destroy it, lest they incur the wrath of the ghost. Her portrait was given to the local historical society's museum. The Dutchess's ghost never again knocked on the living room door and, as far as anyone knows, has never descended again from her portrait. Perhaps Dutchess Emily's ghost was enjoying the admiration of strangers in her new surroundings.

The Blood Won't Wash Off

Normally it is not good news for the owner when a house is condemned to make way for a highway widening. But in the case of an old house in Machias, it was, as this house was unrentable and unsaleable as well. There was a good reason why the owner was glad to see it demolished—it was haunted.

Not only was the house haunted, but it was home to a very unsettling ghost indeed. The "purple lady" was notorious in the neighborhood. So many people claimed to have seen her that no one, absolutely no one, would buy or rent the house, which stood derelict for years until the highway project destroyed it.

The purple lady, the story goes, was a transparent specter wearing a long, old-fashioned floor length gown of deep purple. She walked, or rather floated, across the floor of the old house, but about six inches above the surface. The ghostly figure held her hands out in front of her and repeatedly washed them in an enameled tin washbasin hovering before her without any visible support, while lamenting in a low voice. Some who've met this ghost claim that her hands were covered in blood, while others say her hands were clean.

"The blood, Oh the blood!" moaned the purple-hued spirit. "The blood won't wash off!" At one point, frustrated by his inability to rent or sell the house, the owner called in an amateur ghost hunter. Was there a way to persuade the ghost to leave?

The ghost hunter spent one unnerving evening in the haunted house, with two results. First, she did communicate with the purple lady. Second, she gave up ghost hunting permanently.

The ghost, she reported, was that of a midwife who had lived in Machias more than a century before. She had taken great pride in helping mothers deliver healthy babies. But on one occasion, she had been pressured to use her knowledge and skills to terminate an unwanted pregnancy. This was very much against her religion and professional ethics, but times were tough and she really needed the money to feed her own large family.

And so, reluctantly, she was persuaded to perform an abortion. She did it, but the stain on her conscience was transformed into bloodstains on her hands that would not wash off. Has the purple lady finally found peace, now that the scene of her crime no longer exists? One can pray that her spirit finds rest.

The Devil and the Painter

Up in Eastport, the easternmost point in the nation, there is an old legend about the devil and the housepainter. It seems that the house-painter, whom we'll call Fred, was a very unpleasant character. He beat his wife and children, and he drank as often as he could afford it. He wasn't a particularly busy painter, which was fine with him, as he had little ambition beyond tossing back the next drink. Not surprisingly, he had no friends. Also not surprisingly, he was one of those not-so-bright fellows who thought himself quite clever.

It was clear to everyone, even Fred, that he was on his way to an invitation from Satan to spend eternity in hell—an invitation he couldn't refuse. Fred had no known virtues, plenty of bad habits, and was never known to pray or attend church services. When drunk, he'd cynically observe to acquaintances that he planned to repent and ask God's forgiveness at the very last minute, just before the devil showed up to claim his soul. Of course, when the devil was present, it would be too late for repentance.

Sure enough, as Fred lay in a stupor on a barroom floor, the devil showed up. "That sharp pain you are about to feel in your chest is your fatal heart attack, Fred," smiled Satan. "I need a painter down in hell to freshen things up—the smoke from all the hellfires makes my home dingy, and the Missus is complaining again."

"No! Not yet!" begged Fred, scheming to buy time in which to repent and escape the devil's clutches. Knowing that the devil would favor Fred doing yet more evil on earth, Fred said he needed a week in which to beat his wife and children some more. "Done," agreed the devil, "one week."

Now, Fred being the lazy, lying procrastinator that he was, that week went by without his making his peace with the Almighty. The devil caught up with him by the bridge on a moonless night. "Come with me," said the devil. "The Missus is getting impatient about that redecorating you're going to do for us." Thinking fast, Fred said, "How about we have a drink together in the tavern? It will be thirsty work down in hell, and besides, the preachers claim that the tavern is the gateway to hell anyhow. But I've no money. Could I borrow a dollar from you?"

"Well, I don't carry money with me," replied Old Nick, "as I've no need of it in hell."

"Why not change yourself into a silver dollar?" suggested Fred. "I'll buy us two drinks and then you can change back into your present form."

This appealed to the devil's satanic sense of humor, and so a shiny new dollar suddenly lay in Fred's hand. Fred quickly popped the coin into a small pocket purse he'd gotten from his saintly mother—a purse embroidered with the sign of the cross. The devil, powerless against the holy cross, bargained desperately with Fred. "Let me out," he begged, "and by all that is unholy I'll instruct hell's gatekeepers not to let you in! I'll do without the new paint job."

Fred thought it over and decided that it was a good deal. He opened the purse, the devil departed, and Fred considered himself a shrewd man. Cockily, Fred never did bother repenting of his sins and, inevitably, found himself at the pearly gates of heaven. But, as an unrepentant sinner with a long list of grievous offenses against the will of heaven, Fred was denied entrance into paradise. Saint Peter suggested that he apply to hell. But there, true to the devil's word, the keepers barred him from the devil's domain. Fred's spirit was condemned to wander aimlessly about the universe, forever lonely, cold, and forgotten.

Incidentally, without the redecorating talents of Fred, the devil's abode looks as dingy as hell.

Worship Money, Worship the Devil

There are several versions of an old New England folktale about a money lender in league with the devil. One such story concerns a greedy man of Eastport, who came to grief through his worship of money.

Simon Bancroft was his name, and money lending was his game. Even before his career as a money lender, Simon was notoriously tight with money. Now Maine is not the easiest place to make a living, and most folks in the Pine Tree State are careful with money, but with Simon, hoarding money was an unhealthy obsession; especially unhealthy for Simon's wife. She got pneumonia one winter. Simon's stingy use of firewood may have contributed to that. Simon wouldn't send for a doctor, as doctors, as well as medicine, cost money. When the poor woman died, Simon ordered the cheapest coffin available. His wife was buried without a church service, as Simon understood that the clergy usually received a small donation for their services. Needless to say, no headstone marked the grave; a useless expense, said Simon.

This truly mean behavior earned Simon an admirer. Satan was impressed, so much so that he sought Simon out as a prime candidate to spend eternity in hell. The devil invited Simon Bancroft to have a few drinks in the tavern, at the devil's expense of course. Satan explained to Simon that he was looking for some sound investments in these parts and thought Simon had management talents he could use.

Would Simon be interested in owning a slave ship? (This was before the Civil War, of course.) Simon rejected the idea, explaining that folks in Maine were strongly opposed to slavery, did not own slaves, and thus there was no market for slaves. Satan was pleased to hear the objections based on economic issues alone, with no mention of moral concerns. Simon was Satan's kind of man!

"How about setting up an office as a usurer?" asked the Devil. "Usurers are among my best agents on earth. My best friends are those who value money above all else." Simon's eyes glittered at the prospect of extorting high interest and driving folks into hopeless and demeaning bankruptcy. "I'll supply the capital," said the Prince of Darkness, "and you'll supply the ruthless management—we'll be a winning team!"

And so, Bancroft and Company Moneylenders was opened, backed by a chest full of the devil's gold. Simon quickly built a reputation as the lender of last resort: When the banks refused to lend, Simon opened his money chest. Simon gleefully seized houses, farms, businesses, and fishing boats from creditors whose poor judgment, inadequate management skills, or plain bad luck rendered them unable to pay the ruinously high interest demanded.

Simon put in long hours at his desk, a great leather-bound accounting book at his elbow, and an iron money chest at his feet. The money piled up, and Simon acquired many valuable properties through foreclosures. He became a hated man, which didn't bother him at all. Friendless but rich suited him fine.

One day, the story goes, Simon's best client came to his office. The man, once wealthy and powerful, was in tears. A financial panic had swept across the whole country. Banks had failed and money was in short supply. This man's savings had been wiped out when the local bank closed its doors. Couldn't Simon extend the loan for another month? Or even a week? After all, the two had done a lot of business together over the years, greatly enriching the money lender.

Simon's temper flared. He was not in business to help old associates, he was in business to make money. "Not a month, not a week, not a day!" he thundered, "your time is up, your time is come!"

"It's your time that is come!" roared a loud voice from the street. "Your time is up Simon Bancroft." Simon's door was flung open, revealing a frightening sight. A shiny black carriage, drawn by a pair of black horses, stood at his door. The devil himself, dressed all in black as a coachman, dragged Simon to the coach. "Your time is up, Simon. You've ruined every business, bankrupted every man of substance, foreclosed on every profitable farm, and motivated many suicides. You've wrecked this economy, and your usefulness is at an end."

The black carriage sped away, bearing Simon Bancroft straight to hell. Curiously, when the townsfolk at last were brave enough to enter Bancroft and Company, they found an amazing sight. The great ledger in which Simon kept his records was entirely blank. The folio of mortgages and promissory notes contained only ashes. The great iron money chest was filled with sawdust. Nothing was left of Simon's business. His money had vanished, as had Simon.

North Woods

THIS VERY LARGE REGION IN SQUARE MILES ALSO IS MAINE'S SMALLEST in population. All of Maine inland from tidewater is considered the interior. This is where the "Pine Tree State" earns its nickname, for the North Woods contains few people except in the famous potato-growing area of the Aroostook Valley.

The Ghost of the Gold-Finder

The little community of Norridgewock was haunted for decades by a peculiar ghost who walked along slowly, head bent toward the ground, carrying a long stick horizontal to the ground. The stick is a magic divining rod, and the ghost is that of the infamous gold-finder, Joe Lambert.

Lambert and his sons were lumberjacks. They worked hard enough, but it was seasonal work, and the Lamberts were poor. Not that poverty was unusual among lumberjacks—it wasn't. But suddenly, the Lamberts were rich. Really rich. They quit their jobs. They bought new horses and good clothes and began riding about the countryside spending time and money freely in taverns. They generously bought rounds of drinks for all and would smile mysteriously when questioned about the source of their newfound fortune.

Gradually, they leaked their secret to their new friends. They had found a gold mine. Not just one gold mine, actually, but dozens of places that yielded the glittering metal. How did they do it? Father and sons had discovered how to "witch" an ordinary maple branch into a magical divining rod. By holding the divining rod out in front of them as they walked slowly along, the Lamberts could locate gold when the divining rod twitched downward. Gold, they pointed out, was very heavy. Its unusual weight would pull the divining rod downward as the rod passed over a deposit of gold.

Their excited, and somewhat inebriated, listeners were all ears. Could they too learn how to "witch up" some gold? Could they obtain divining rods as powerful as that of the Lamberts?

Well, yes, said Joe Lambert. He could sell a divining rod to them. In fact, he'd sell his own, proven divining rod to a group of friends, as he and his sons wished to retire from the gold-finding business. They had plenty to live on and were tired of walking about in the woods at night, holding onto their divining rod.

The price was high, understandably, so a large group of would-be gold finders pooled their savings to acquire the divining rod and its secrets. A stout maple branch must be held tightly in front of them in as straight a line as possible. This was to be done only around midnight of a full moon. The full moon, explained Joe Lambert, added to the gravitational pull of the gold on the divining rod. So scientific!

A week before the next full moon the Lamberts handed over their divining rod to the group of investors. "Good luck!" said Joe and his sons as they rode away. Now, of course, diligent strolls through the countryside with the magical divining rod at midnight on full moons produced nothing but sore arms and much frustration. Gradually, it occurred to the investors that they'd been tricked out of a lot of money.

The group of investors was transformed into an angry mob. One moonless night, they were lucky enough to find Joe Lambert, in a tavern, telling his tale of finding gold. At the following dawn, Joe was found dead, a stout maple branch thrust through his heart. It was a divining rod of death.

For many years afterward, folks around Norridgewock swore they'd seen a ghostly figure strolling about, holding a rod out in front of him, looking for gold. And finding death, at midnight, on a full moon.

The Ghost Who Flinches at Gunfire

The little town of Sangerville, about thirty-five miles northwest of Bangor, is occasionally visited by an unusual ghost—one who visibly flinches at the sound of gunfire. During hunting season, the sound of gunshots is hardly unusual. Anyone living in the Maine woods knows how gunfire reverberates through the forest as hunters from near and far seek their quota of deer, rabbits, moose, or even bear, not to mention ducks and geese.

The ghost is that of an elderly man, distinguished in appearance, prosperously dressed in late Victorian attire. The phantom strolls along the leafy streets of the little town, a tranquil expression on his face until a gunshot rings out in the nearby woods. At that, the ghost becomes agitated, trembles, and then disappears.

Why is this disembodied spirit so negatively affected by the sound of gunfire? Maybe it is a guilty conscience, for some believe that the ghost is that of Sangerville's most famous son, the inventor Hiram Maxim.

Young Hiram, born in 1840, decided early that he wanted to become an inventor. His efforts included an automatic steam pump, vacuum pumps, a locomotive headlight, and an engine governor. Hiram Maxim was rich and successful already before he turned his attention to developing his most famous, and deadliest invention, the Maxim gun. The Maxim gun was a rapid-fire machine gun—the first of its kind. Hiram was living in England at the time and was able to convince Edward, Prince of Wales, that his gun would revolutionize warfare. The gun went into production, and Hiram was knighted by the British in 1901 when his gun helped them win the Boer War in South Africa.

The Maxim gun did indeed change warfare. When both sides used it during World War I, the Maxim gun literally mowed down thousands of soldiers a day. Hiram had hoped that his super-efficient gun would make war unthinkable; instead, it made war horrific. Hiram Maxim lived long enough (he died in 1916) to see his invention become the supreme killing machine of modern warfare, at least up until the First World War.

Troubled by nightmares of mass killings before his death, Hiram's ghost now winces at every gunshot it hears. Unintentionally, his fame and wealth rested upon heaps of dead soldiers. Incidentally, the name of his hometown, Sangerville, is derived from the French word, sangre, meaning blood. Sangerville could be translated as "Bloodtown."

Big Squaw Mountain's Eternal Flame

Moosehead Lake, the largest in Maine, is flanked by rugged, mountainous terrain. Near the lake is Big Squaw Mountain (3,267 feet) and, actually in the lake, is Mount Kineo (1,806 feet). These two mountains are linked in Indian legend, a legend that explains the mysterious light often seen flickering atop Big Squaw.

The legend is that, a long time ago, a great warrior named Kineo lived on the mountain that now bears his name. He had retreated to the mountain in the lake as a self-imposed exile from his tribe, for Kineo had a notoriously bad temper. He just couldn't seem to get along with others. His great courage and excellent hunting abilities would have made him a natural leader, except for his quick anger at any questioning of his decisions by his fellow tribesmen. His temper isolated him from the social life of the group, and he withdrew in anger to his mountain in the lake.

One evening he saw, over the black waters of Moosehead Lake, a bright flame atop Big Squaw Mountain to his south. He decided to investigate. When Kineo reached the summit of Big Squaw, he found there the embers of a great bonfire. Beside the ashes lay his own mother, almost dead of exhaustion. She had followed him to beg him to return to his tribe and return to her. She died in his arms, entreating him to change his ways, curb his temper, and rejoin his people.

Kineo did as she asked with her dying breath and became a great chief of his people. And the beacon lit by his own mother atop Big Squaw Mountain still flickers, though no fire actually burns there, reminding people to control their tempers if they would be leaders. And listen to your mother, too.

The Chief Who Spoke with the Birds

Norridgewock, far up the Kennebec River near Skowhegan, is the site of an ancient Indian village. It once was a very important place, being on the Kennebec-Chaudiers Rivers' route by which Indians traveled from the St. Lawrence Valley to the Maine coast.

The Wabanaki Indians preferred to travel by canoe, and so rivers were their highways. But these interior passages needed to be connected by portages—overland paths from one river's headwaters to another's. Laying out the portages was tricky work and required someone with a great sense of direction and awareness of their surroundings.

The legend is that a great chief, Waban, whose name means "dawn" or "morning" could find his way through trackless wilderness. Waban never got lost in the woods. Why not? Waban had a secret. He could talk to the birds, and the birds would fly high enough to spot distant landmarks, then fly ahead, leading Waban to his objective. Waban blazed trails with ease, thanks to his feathered friends.

Waban, it is claimed, had such great powers that he never died. He still walks through the forests, clearing paths for his people, and assisting those who are lost.

If you get lost in the Maine woods, just whistle like a bird and follow the answering birdcalls. Waban's spirit will lead you home.

The Captain Lost His Head

The tiny town of Naples lies on Long Lake, about twenty miles southwest of Auburn. It has a haunted house, and this ghost is that of a man, dressed as an early-nineteenth-century sea captain; he has no head.

After the captain was beheaded in far off China, his body was shipped home for burial. But no one ever found his head. The story is that those who beheaded him kept his head and placed it on exhibit in a Chinese temple as a warning not to violate their religious beliefs.

And so, the headless phantom walks the rooms of his once fine mansion. The gold braid on his shoulders is still bright, as are the gold buttons on his dark blue uniform. The ghost jingles some gold coins in his pockets. How he lost his head has a lot do with gold.

Just what is the ghost of a sea captain doing so far from the Atlantic coast? It is his ancestral home. The land had been given to John Hill, as a bonus for his service in the American Revolution. The veteran fathered two sons, one of whom became Capt. Charles Hill, who engaged in the clipper ship trade with the Orient. Now, believe it or not, the clever Yankee traders carried ice, cut from winter lakes and ponds and insulated in sawdust, to China. Wealthy Chinese welcomed the blocks of ice to cool their drinks, exchanging tea, silks, and fine porcelain for Maine ice. Many grew rich in this trade, for the ice cost only a few pennies a ton to those who cut and hauled it.

But Captain Hill's great wealth came from more than just honest trade. The rumor was that the Captain and his crew, armed with sabers and pistols, entered the inner, most sacred rooms of a Chinese temple and stole several large idols. These idols, it turned out, were solid gold. The captain netted $300,000 from his share of the loot and retired to Naples. He added a huge new wing to his father's house and filled it with expensive furniture and rare luxuries.

After building his new house, the captain made a series of ill-advised investments and lost much of his new wealth. He decided to voyage to China once more and steal more of the fabulous wealth of the great temple.

But this time the temple's priests were armed with great swords. They recognized the captain and decapitated him. That is how the headless ghost returned home, endlessly jingling a few gold coins in his pockets, regretting the day he violated the sanctuary of that temple so far from Maine.

The Bewitched Axe

Deep in the Maine woods, around the logging town of Millinocket, they tell the tale of the magical axe of Robert Cartier.

Cartier was one of many French Canadians who had come south to work in Maine's logging industry. They were known as robust, hard-working, and to tell the truth, hard-drinking and hard-cussing men.

Cartier was as big and brawny as any, but he had a lazy streak. He was fond of long lunch hours and afternoon naps under a tree. His worst characteristic, though, was a genuine fondness for brawling in low-down bars. Robert liked nothing better than knocking heads and breaking noses. Another favorite sport was seducing the wives and daughters of other loggers—a pastime sure to stir up more fights. In short, Robert Cartier was a world-class troublemaker.

And that brought him to the attention of the patron saint of human misery, Satan. Satan met Cartier one dark night. "Bob," said Satan, who always liked to put his admirers at ease, "I've got a proposition for you. Save your energy for fighting and mischief; I'll give you a magical axe that will work while you whistle." "Done!" said Robert. Satan gave him the axe. "Just whistle a peppy tune, and the axe will go to work, your work," said Satan.

It worked; the axe did, that is. While Cartier relaxed under a tree, whistling a merry tune, the axe hacked down trees by the dozen. Cartier's ample earnings from his busy axe were spent in saloons, leading many of Robert's friends to a life of drunkenness and debauchery. The axe may be cutting wood for Robert, but it surely was doing the devil's own work as well.

Late in life, Robert Cartier began to worry about his future in the afterlife. Wouldn't a life of sin doom his immortal soul? But, before he could reform, Cartier was found in the woods, beheaded by one great cut of his bewitched axe.

The axe was never found. There are those who believe that, on moonless nights, the axe can be heard cutting trees in the darkness all by itself. If someone is whistling, that is.

Be careful about whistling in the dark in the Maine woods.

The Indian Princess of Lightning

Mount Katahdin is to the Wabanaki Indians what Mount Olympus was to the ancient Greeks—the home of the gods. It is a very impressive peak, rising over 4,500 feet above its base on the banks of the Penobscot River. It is the highest mountain in Maine and always has been a very special place in the hearts of the region's first people.

In the epic story of Kinaldo, the Indian brave is fascinated by the brilliant beauty of the Princess Lightning, whose shining face he has seen on storm clouds. Kinaldo leaves home to seek Lightning, finding her high on the slopes of Katahdin. The princess falls in love with the handsome man who had the courage to come to her in all her terrible glory. Lightning persuades her father, the Mountain King Spirit, to throw a wedding feast for the couple at a great hall deep under the mountain. At the feast, so goes the story, Lightning slips a magic potion to Kinaldo that makes him forget his past. This frees Kinaldo of any regrets about leaving his people.

But one day Kinaldo is awakened from a dream in which his little sister, Winona, has never stopped praying that she could see him once again. The power of the innocent girl's prayers overcomes the magic potion's effect: Kinaldo remembers that he was a mortal man.

Kinaldo is determined to go down from the mountain and visit his family. The Mountain King and Princess Lightning try to dissuade him, "Once you have lived among the gods, you can't go back," the Mountain King warns. "You cannot live among men!"

Kinaldo insists, and he goes down among his people. A great storm develops over Katahdin. The mighty thunder calls him home to the mountain. A terrified Kinaldo goes to the base of the great mountain where, suddenly, a blinding streak of lightning reaches down and seizes him.

When the storm clears, Kinaldo's dead body lay as asleep at the foot of the mountain. To this day, it is said, the Wabenaki hide from the thunder warriors and try not to stare at the fabled beauty of Princess Lightning, for hers is a fatal attraction.

The Son of the Magic Mountain

Mount Katahdin, at 5,267 feet above sea level, is the highest point in Maine; in fact, its Indian name means "highest land." There are several Wabanaki Indian legends about Katahdin, which was, and is, a very special place to Maine's first people.

One legend has it that the magic mountain once fathered a child by an Indian maiden. It seems that a young girl, growing up in the shadow of Katahdin, was fascinated by the mountain. To her, Mount Katahdin symbolized great strength, power, and masculine beauty.

She fantasized that, someday, the spirit of the mountain would come to her and make her his bride.

One day she went off into the woods at the foot of the mountain to pick blueberries, which still grow wild there. She failed to return. The whole tribe went searching for her, but to no avail. Eventually, her people had to give up and accept her mysterious disappearance.

Three years later, she reappeared as mysteriously as she had disappeared. She had with her a beautiful baby boy. Curiously, the child had eyebrows of stone—stone the same color as that of Katahdin. She refused to name the boy's father. Despite nagging from the tribe's gossips, she would not reveal what had happened during here three-year absence.

The boy grew up, stronger and more handsome every day. It soon became apparent that he possessed awesome, supernatural powers. If he pointed at a bird, fish, or animal, it died. The kind-hearted boy soon learned to use this miraculous power sparingly, for he had great respect for all life.

Then came a terrible winter, in which the tribe suffered greatly. Game was scarce. The few deer about were very fleet of foot and hard to kill. The people began to starve, so the boy with magical powers used his supernatural abilities to kill enough game to provide food for all. He and he alone prevented disaster.

But the tribe's gratitude was soon overshadowed by malicious gossip. The tongues were wagging about just who the boy must be. Exactly how had his mother come to bear such a magical child? His mother was harassed endlessly by insinuations about his paternity. They forgot how much they owed to the miraculous hunting abilities of this boy and instead made cruel jokes about his eyebrows of stone.

At last, tired and angered by the tribe's ingratitude, his mother burst forth, "Fools! Ingrates! Your cruelty and folly will doom you! You must know that this is the true son of Katahdin, sent to save you and your children from famine. You have forsaken him!" And with that, the woman and her godlike son departed.

From that time forward, the Wabanaki were a doomed people. The white men stole their hunting grounds and the once-proud "people of the dawn" almost disappeared. Ingratitude is a terrible thing.

The Logger Who Befriended the Devil

In the tiny town of Dyer Brook, they tell the story of the logger who made friends with the devil. This was back in the days when Dyer Brook, near Houlton on the Canadian border, was a thriving logging center.

Loggers were a tough lot. They needed to be, as riding a bunch of logs down the river to a sawmill was a lot harder work, and more dangerous, than riding with a herd of cattle on the plains. Floating logs, raging along in a strong current, had a nasty habit of turning over in the water without warning. Woe to the logger who tried to go out on the floating logs to free up a jam, for falling between the heavy, careening logs was an unpleasant way to die. No doubt about it, log driving out on the river demanded a fearless acrobat capable of leaping from one rolling churning log to another, with the brute strength to break up a jam and get the logs rolling again. You might say that job required a devil-may-care attitude.

Such a log driver was the legendary Jack the Ripper. The other Jack the Ripper, the one in London, was a mild-mannered gent compared to Dyer Brook's profane log-driving man.

There was a belief among loggers that if a man were to go to the same place on the riverbanks for seven nights at the same hour, and ask to speak to the devil, the evil one would appear on the seventh night and talk with the man. Few wished to meet the devil in person, on the reasonable assumption that this was risky business for one's soul.

One night in a bar, Jack the Ripper, having drunk more than his customary full bottle of whiskey, accepted a challenge from an equally drunken mate. He would speak with the devil. Could the devil be any tougher than a log driver in the north woods of Maine?

Having fulfilled the seven night's requirements, Jack suddenly was face-to-face with you-know-who. Satan turned out to be grateful for the company of such a hard-drinking, hard-living, hard-cussing man as a Maine log driver and talked in a friendly fashion with Jack. "Jack," advised the devil, "stay off the logs tomorrow. There will be a terrible accident."

Jack ignored the warning and jumped carelessly from log to log, determined to do his job. As he did so, a flaming red pickaxe reared up between the tumbling logs. This time, Jack heeded the warning and quickly lept to shore. And just in time too, as three men died on the logjam that day.

Even afterward, folks stayed well clean of Jack the Ripper. Any friend of the devil was a man to avoid. Jack never did have an accident out on the logs. Maybe it was just the devil's luck.

Witching the Weather

Out in the Kennebec River near the town of Hallowell, just south of Augusta, is a huge rock known as Mill Rock. According to a local legend, it washed into the river during a fearful thunderstorm—a storm "conjured up" by a local man who was a witch.

The story is that one Uncle Kaler, an old man of Finnish background, had some magical powers. But he always used his powers for good, not evil. Uncle Kaler could make amulets that brought good luck to sailors. He could cure a farmer's cattle that had been bewitched. His love potions brought many happy couples together and became his specialty. Oh, and he could make either good or bad weather to order.

This wizard lived by a quiet millbrook just off the river road. One spring evening there was an anxious knock at his door. A distraught young man stood there alongside a truly lovely young lady. "Please help us!" he begged of Uncle Kaler. "My love and I are on our way to Augusta to be married, but her family disapproves of the match. Listen, you can hear the hounds they've set on us!" And the wizard could hear baying hounds and pounding horses' hooves in the distance. "Could you conjure up a storm that will slow the pursuit?" asked the girl.

Uncle Kaler was a romantic old fellow and much in sympathy with the couple who were so obviously in love. He went back into his house and foraged around in his box of tricks. He gave the young man a small leather bag and instructed him to pour the contents on the road between himself and the pursuers. "Go in peace," said the wizard.

The young lovers did as they were told. No sooner had they left Uncle Kaler's house to hurry along the road when a tremendous thunderstorm blew up. Lightning sent huge trees down across the road, and torrential rains obliterated any scent of the fleeing lovers. Heavy rains washed a huge boulder down the mountainside, smashing a local mill and temporarily blocking the river road before washing into the river.

The young couple made it safely to Augusta for their wedding. The mammoth boulder in the river is proof, the locals claim, of the huge storm conjured up by Uncle Kaler, that old romantic, to help young lovers in distress.

The Disappointed Ghost

The ghost is that of a distinguished-looking Victorian gentlemen, dressed all in the severe black formal wear of the late nineteenth century. Although in life the man accomplished a great deal and was one of Maine's most famous native sons at the time, the ghost looks the picture of dejection, regrets, and depression. There is a good reason for this spirit to be so morose, for he very nearly was president of the United States. But it was not to be.

President Hannibal Hamlin, the title sounded grand, but it never happened. Hamlin was born in 1809, the same year as Abraham Lincoln, in the tiny Maine town of Paris. Like Lincoln, his onetime hero and friend, Hannibal was a poor boy who worked his way out of poverty by educating himself in the law, becoming a successful lawyer before entering politics.

Folks in Maine did not hold with slavery. The few African Americans in the Pine Tree State were free men who worked hard and enjoyed the respect of their neighbors. Hamlin was elected to the Maine legislature as a Democrat who opposed slavery. When he went to Washington as a U.S. senator in 1848, he split with his fellow Democrats on the slavery issue, becoming a strong believer in the necessity of emancipation. Abraham Lincoln was a hero to Hannibal Hamlin, and so Hannibal was deeply honored to be asked to run as Lincoln's vice-presidential candidate in 1860.

Hamlin was frustrated by the vice presidency, as indeed were most holders of that office. A loyal supporter of Lincoln, whom he considered a friend, Hamlin was most unpleasantly surprised when the Republican National Convention in 1864 dropped him off the ticket. Abraham Lincoln had said that he would leave the selection of a running mate up to the convention. The rumor was, however, that Lincoln believed that the ticket would be strengthened more by choosing Andrew Johnson as the vice-presidential candidate. Johnson, a "War Democrat" had been the only southern senator to remain loyal to the union. Lincoln believed that a "national unity" ticket with a southern Democrat would have the best chance of victory. And so Hannibal Hamlin was dumped from the ticket. An embittered Hamlin returned to his home in Bangor that he had purchased while vice president, and the Lincoln-Johnson ticket went on to victory—a victory that Hamlin helped secure by loyally campaigning for Lincoln.

Imagine Hannibal Hamlin's tremendous sense of outraged disappointment when Andrew Johnson, vice president for only a month, was thrust into the presidency by an assassin's bullet in Lincoln's brain. But for Lincoln's calculated decision to replace him on the ticket, Hannibal Hamlin of Maine would have been the president of the United States.

And so Hamlin's ghost roams his Bangor home, head hanging low, sad eyes staring into infinity as he realizes just how close he came to the highest office in the land. His is a quiet, non-threatening ghost who simply evaporates should he become aware of a living person near him. Poor Hannibal—once only a heartbeat, or a bullet, away from being President.

The UFO and the Preacher's Son

Shortly after World War II, a UFO was reported near the town of Presque Isle up in the Aroostook Valley where most of Maine's potatoes are grown. Old timers there are still divided in their opinions as to whether a genuine UFO really was seen there, or whether there was some other explanation for the fantastic story told by a preacher's son.

The fact that he was a preacher's son was used to support their beliefs by both sides on this controversy. Believers in UFOs asserted that being a preacher's son and reared in a household of piety and strict observance of the Ten Commandments should make the word of this lad more reliable than most. Who but a preacher's son would be more familiar with the commandment forbidding bearing false witness? On the other hand, those inclined to doubt the UFO report from the preacher's son also cite his father's occupation as a reason for disbelief.

The Presque Isle preacher's offspring had observed, while on a solitary camping and hunting trip out in the woods, a celestial object traveling so quickly that it created its own whirling sound. It appeared from a cloud, surrounded by flashes like lightning. In the midst of a brilliant light, it glowed like molten metal. Out of this fiery sphere came four creatures that looked, at first glance, like men. However, as they got closer it could be seen that each visitor had four faces and four wings. Their legs were straight, and their feet looked like cow's hooves. Under each wing they had humanlike hands. These alien creatures moved straight ahead without turning as they went. Their bodies glowed with bright light as though they were on fire, but they did not burn. They could move as fast as lightning.

Fascinating, said the believers. After all, he is a preacher's son, so he wouldn't lie. Fascinating indeed, said the skeptics. They pointed out that, as a preacher's son, he would have heard or read about precisely those images in the Bible—in the first chapter of the Book of Ezekiel, to be exact.

Yes, this description does appear in Ezekiel. Which brings up another question: Could the ancient Israelites, during their captivity in Babylon have actually witnessed aliens emerging from as UFO? Read Ezekiel for yourself.

The Drummer's Ghost

A judge's family in the state capital of Augusta once was haunted by the ghost of a man sent to jail by the judge. This happened around the time of the Civil War and is a frightening example of the activities of a poltergeist. In German, poltergeist means "boisterous spirit"; poltergeists cause physical objects to move in plain view of those being haunted.

The story is that an old man, an army veteran of the War of 1812, was making a nuisance of himself by begging in the streets. He had been a drummer boy in that war and knew a larger repertoire of military tattoos—styled drumbeats that, like bugle calls, communicated orders to troops on the battlefield where a human voice would be unintelligible. He thought of himself as a street entertainer, though many who dropped a few coins in his old hat at his feet doubtless hoped that their gifts would encourage silence rather than more drumrolls.

After repeatedly refusing to move on after being warned, the old man was arrested as a public nuisance and brought before a judge. It was clear that the old veteran was not mentally competent, so the judge ordered him sent to jail, as much to ensure the old man a warm bed and hot meals as to protect the eardrums of the citizenry.

The confused old drummer was bitter. He believed that he'd only used his one talent to coax a few pennies from passersby, and he felt betrayed. Late one night, he managed to hang himself in his cell. That was when the trouble started.

Late that same night, the judge and his family were awakened by loud drumming that seemed to circle their house like a parade. The drumbeats did not cease until dawn, when the judge found the old man's battered drum on his front porch. No one knew how it got there. The angry judge ordered the drum burned, which it was.

Later that day, rhythmic tapping was heard in the judge's kitchen. On investigating the sound, the judge's family was horrified to see a wooden spoon beating on an empty pot—but no one was there. At the dinner table, silverware began tapping on water glasses while candlesticks beat upon the table, again with no human hands involved. At night, unseen knuckles rapped on the headboards of beds as doors repeatedly opened and then slammed shut.

These mysterious drumbeat sounds plagued the judge until his early death some months later. His family swore that, as the judge lay dying, they could hear the slow, measured beat of a muffled drum, as in a funeral precession.

God Rest His Soul

A clergyman who wishes to remain anonymous related this interesting experience. He had just been appointed vicar of an old church in Bangor. He was about to leave the church following choir practice one evening when a middle-aged lady, a stranger to him, approached. She was visibly agitated and quite anxious to speak with him. She asked him to come quickly to an address nearby. "A gentleman is dying there," she said, "and he is very concerned about the state of his soul. He really needs to speak with you and confess his sins before he dies." How could a conscientious minister of the church refuse such a summons, especially as delivered by such a sincerely concerned lady?

The lady had a cab waiting and urged great haste. "He will die soon," she said. "Please reassure him of God's love and forgiveness." After a short drive, the minister was delivered to a large, imposing house. "Hurry!" urged the lady. "God rest his soul." The vicar sprang from the taxi and went up the steps to the front door. A young woman calmly answered the door. "Does Mister Chambers live here?" asked the vicar. "Yes, but what is this about?" was her answer. "This lady told me that I should see him," said the clergyman, who, turning toward the street, then realized that the lady had disappeared. "Well, I don't know who sent you," said the young woman, "but my father wouldn't want to turn you away. He hasn't been feeling well recently and would appreciate some company."

The minister went into the living room where an elderly man, in apparent good health, sat on a couch. "I haven't been to church in a while," he said. "It was good of you to stop by." The gentleman had not sent for the minister, but said that he was glad to see him, as he wanted to discuss something that was troubling him. In his youth he had done some things of which he was ashamed. Could he be forgiven? The minister listened and counseled him for an hour. It was agreed that the old man would attend church the next day, and they would continue their discussion afterward.

The man did not appear. When the minister went to his house, he discovered a family in mourning. The old man had died unexpectedly the previous evening, only ten minutes after the clergyman had left. Would the minister go up to the bedroom where the deceased lay? After saying a brief prayer over the body, the minister saw a large photo of the lady who had summoned him the night before. "Who is that?" he queried. "That is my mother," replied the daughter. "She died fifteen years ago."

The Millinocket Devil-Fish

Up in the north woods of Maine, they often tell "tall tales," just as they do in the great north woods of the upper Midwest, where the legends of Paul Bunyan and his blue ox were born. There is an old-time, half-forgotten tale of a monstrous devil-fish that might have been Satan himself with gills and fins. It is a story that cautions against breaking the Sabbath, for that was the ill-considered act that produced the monster.

It seems that one of Millinocket's more ornery lumberjacks was a man named Jack Johnston. Jack never was known to cross the threshold of a church. He openly disdained religious practices and beliefs and considered the tradition of keeping the Sabbath holy to be just another rule made to be broken.

Jack was a rarity among fishermen—an avid fisherman who never had learned the great lesson of successful fishing—patience. Impatience and fishing do not go well together. Jack went fishing one Sunday when religious folks were in church, and even not-so-religious folks were reluctant to publicly break the long tradition of not going sportfishing on Sundays. He was having no luck. His bait was taken repeatedly by crafty fish who avoided getting hooked. Jack's temper flared, and he began cursing the fish, the sport of fishing, fishermen, pious churchgoers, the Sabbath tradition, the community of Millinocket, the state of Maine, and for good measure, the devil himself.

After cursing the devil at great length and in highly colorful language, Jack at long last felt a firm tug on his line. When he reeled in his catch, it was the ugliest looking fish he'd ever seen. It looked more like a snake with a mouthful of razorlike fangs, bulging red eyes, and a long, writhing black body covered in a foul-smelling slime.

Disgusted, Jack threw the nasty creature into a nearby well and forgot about it. Then strange events began to take place in the vicinity of the well. Local people swore that they saw the snake-fish crawl out of the well at night to feed on chickens, piglets, cats, and dogs, even an occasional sheep. As time went on, people began tossing sacrifices down the well to placate the beast, hoping to forestall its nightly raids on local farms. It started with a ham or leg of lamb, then progressed to whole deer or cows. It was as if the devil himself had responded to Jack's string of curses while fishing on the Sabbath.

The monster's appetite was growing even beyond whole live steers. Something had to be done. The people appealed to Jack. It was Jack Johnston's fault, they argued, that the evil creature lived in the well. He must do something about it.

But how could Jack survive a battle with the fearsome devil-fish? He consulted a witch, who offered the use of an enchanted sword. The sword, she swore, was all-powerful and would slay the monster. There was a condition—after killing the demon fish, Jack must also kill the next living creature to cross his path. Failure to do so would doom Jack's soul into the hands of the devil. The deal was struck.

Craftily, Jack arranged to have a chicken tethered to a bush near the well. After dispatching the monster of the well, Jack would turn to face the chicken and kill it to fulfill his pledge.

Armed with the charmed blade, Jack won his struggle with the devil-fish, as the witch foretold. But, as he turned away from the well, his own father rushed up to embrace the hero of the hour. Jack could not kill his own father, the first living creature he met after slaying the monster. He broke his agreement with the witch and so his soul was claimed by the devil. Think twice before going fishing on the Sabbath.

The Devil Builds a Barn

As folks "down East" in Maine say, you've got to be careful when dealing with the devil. It is tempting to take advantage of the awesome powers of the Lord of the Underworld, but one's immortal soul is at stake. The devil comes out a winner on most of his deals, but now and then, the mortal wins, especially when the devil deals with a crafty old timer from the Pine Tree State.

It seems that a farmer up around Caribou needed a new barn in which to store his potato barrels. He needed that barn very badly, as he just had a shed behind the house for storage. But he had no money to have a barn built. What to do? The old farmer was desperate—so desperate, in fact, that he considered making a pact with the devil.

And sure enough, the Prince of Darkness himself showed up one winter evening. He had a proposition. He'd build a handsome new barn in return for the farmer's soul. Now a man doesn't grow up on a Maine farm without learning how to bargain. The farmer insisted that the barn be built overnight, that the building was completed before the first rooster crowed in the morning.

The devil figured that this was doable, as winter nights in Maine are long, and the devil could work hard and fast when he wanted to. The deal was struck; hands were shaken on it. All night long, the devil worked like, well, like the devil. His hammer flew like lightning as the barn neared completion. An hour before dawn, as only a few roof shingles needed nailing, the farmer crept out to his hen house. There, he made an imitation of crowing. The old rooster answered him, of course. The man got his barn free, and the devil got a free lesson in dealing with those crafty old Maine farmers.

The Spirit of Robin Hood

Everyone has heard of Robin Hood, the legendary outlaw of Sherwood Forest in England. His very name has come to symbolize robbing the rich to give to the poor. Not everyone, however, has heard of Aroostook County's own phantom "Robin Hood," who also gave to the poor while relieving the rich of some of their surplus cash. Maine's own version of Robin Hood was a ghost, or so at least some believe.

One of many stories about this phantom Robin Hood–like character involves the poor widow Lemaire who lived on a farm near Caribou around 1910. Her potato crop had failed, her children were ashamed to go to school because they had no proper shoes, and the mortgage payment was overdue.

One morning a stranger came to her kitchen door. "I've been walking since dawn," he said. "Could I trouble you for a cup of coffee and some breakfast?" Seeing her hesitation, he added, "I can pay for my breakfast." The poor widow made him a tasty omelet. After pouring each of them a second cup of coffee, however, she broke down in tears. "Tell me your troubles," said the stranger, as he counted ten copper pennies out on the table. "The bank manager is coming out here today," she sobbed, "and my mortgage on the farm is due to be paid off, but I've no money—no money at all." "And how much is owed?" he queried. "A thousand dollars," she wailed. Taking a heavy leather pouch from his knapsack, the stranger counted out one hundred gold ten dollar pieces. Over the widow's amazed protests, he assured her that he could, and would, pay off her mortgage so that she and her children wouldn't be evicted. He wrote out a receipt that stated that the banker was handing over the original mortgage agreement and considered it paid off in full "for value received this day from Mrs. Lemaire." "Copy this receipt in your own hand and make sure the banker signs and dates it," he advised, "and when he hands over the mortgage, be sure to burn it."

The stranger took his leave and strolled down the farm lane as the banker drove up in his buggy. The banker, smiling at the thought of acquiring the Lemaire farm for half its actual value, knocked on the door. When the widow handed over the gold coins and requested that he sign a receipt, the man was astounded. "Where did the money come from?" he demanded. "A kind stranger was able to help me—didn't you see him pass you in the lane?" she replied. "I saw no one," he said, surprised.

But his real surprise came when he returned to the bank only to find one hundred copper pennies in his pocket. "But I put a hundred gold ten dollar coins in my pocket—I'm sure of that!" he complained to his lawyer. "How did this happen?" "However it happened," advised the lawyer, "You signed a receipt for 'value received,' and you did get one dollar—so you have no legal recourse."

Meanwhile, back on the farm, Mrs. Lemaire was amazed to discover that the ten copper pennies given her at breakfast were now ten gold ten dollar pieces. Just who was that stranger? And how had the sample receipt he'd written out for her become a blank sheet of paper?

A Dance With Death

This old legend now is half-forgotten, which is understandable considering that it happened back in 1725. It was during the fourth Indian War, which raged across Maine between 1722 and 1726. This war, also known as Lovewell's War, was part of a long struggle between Britain and France for the control of northeastern America. Both sides made alliances with Indian tribes, and both sides paid their Indian allies to bring in scalps of their opponents. In fact, some historians believe that it was the Europeans who introduced Indians to the horrific practice of scalping their enemies.

The legend of the dance with death took place in Fryeburg, the oldest town in Oxford County, which was built on the site of an Indian village called Pequawket. A troop of soldiers from Massachusetts, led by British officers, were camped in town. Some of the town's young women took full advantage of the social opportunities afforded by the presence of so many soldiers. Rachel Adams, the town flirt, decided to "set her cap" for the most eligible bachelor, the English captain of the colonial troops. Captain Sayers was handsome, rich, and equipped with all the social graces. He also was relatively innocent in the ways of coquettish women.

The captain fell deeply in love with Rachel and determined to have her hand in marriage. Rachel in turn swore eternal fealty to her captain, though with less sincerity than he expected. Captain Sayers led an attack on a distant Indian village. When the soldiers returned, they reported their captain missing and presumed dead. Rachel wasted little time in finding a replacement for her captain. Out of sight, out of mind seemed to be her motto. Within two weeks, Rachel had selected her replacement eternal love and planned her wedding. The wedding reception, held at her parents' home, was a great social event, attracting most of the townspeople as well as the soldiers.

The bride and groom had just begun their first dance when the door suddenly flew open. A gust of wind blew out the candles and nearly extinguished the roaring fire in the fireplace. In stomped the most frightening sight anyone there had ever seen. It was Captain Sayers, or rather the rotting corpse of the Captain. His entire scalp was missing—cut off as a trophy by Indians. A large portion of his skull also was missing, and an Indian tomahawk was still buried in his skull. His eyes glowed red with a hellish light. His bloodstained uniform was filthy and torn.

Without a word, the horrific apparition seized Rachel from the arms of her groom and whirled her about in a grotesque waltz, a dance of death. Everyone else stood frozen with fear as the musicians, as though in a trance, mindlessly played waltz after waltz. Finally, the corpse staggered out the door leaving behind Rachel, who collapsed on the floor, her face contorted in fear and loathing. It is said that Rachel never said another word, spending the rest of her life in an insane asylum. Captain Sayers's decomposed body later was found on the distant battlefield where he had fallen. Next to his heart was a white rose he'd plucked from Rachel's bridal bouquet—on that fateful night when he returned from the dead to claim his bride.

The Phantom Train

Up in Maine's great north woods near Moosehead Lake, a few old-timers recall the legend of the phantom train. This train may never have existed, but the folks who saw it, or thought they saw it, swore that it saved their lives. Memories of the phantom train are fading now, as this occurred more than a century ago, in the early 1900s.

Although many outside the state don't realize it, a Canadian railroad runs right across Maine, east to west, in the far north. The Canadian Pacific cuts across Maine on the shortest route connecting Montreal with Saint John, New Brunswick, and on to Halifax, Nova Scotia. This line carries a great deal of freight between these Canadian cities. It was on the Canadian Pacific's route near Moosehead Lake that the phantom train appeared one night in early spring.

A train belonging to the Bangor and Aroostook Railroad was running on the Canadian Pacific's tracks, doing a local run between Jackman and Greenville. Running on another railroad's tracks was done all the time, with permission and properly scheduled to avoid collisions. Late one night in break-up season (when the ice on lakes and rivers begins to melt), the Bangor and Aroostook's weekly freight local was laboring up a grade near the southwestern edge of Moosehead Lake. It was a routine run, one the crew knew by heart.

But this was not to be a routine night, far from it. The men of the train crew were about to have an experience they'd remember to their dying day. It was the night of the phantom train.

The engineer and fireman were relaxing in the locomotive's cab, enjoying for once, as it was a cold night, the warmth of the firebox as it was fed with coal from the tender. In summer, the radiated heat could be brutal, but now it was just cozy.

The faint blast of a far off locomotive's steam whistle broke the silence of the north woods. The engineer leaned out the side window to survey the double tracks ahead, thinking an approaching train was courteously saluting them, but no train was visible coming from the opposite direction. Quickly glancing back as his train entered the gentle curve, the engineer was unpleasantly surprised to see a locomotive headlight following behind on the same track. No other train was scheduled on the track at this hour—how could this be? Worse news—the following train was traveling at a high speed, gaining rapidly on the local freight.

The engineer and fireman agreed that this pursuer must be a "special," an unscheduled extra train. But why had they not been warned? And why was the following train approaching at such a speed as to be dangerously closing the distance between them? The only way to avoid being rear-ended by the recklessly speeding stranger would be to switch to a siding and allow the follower to pass by on the main track. Frantically, they telegraphed ahead to a switchman to throw the switch to a siding they knew lay ahead, just before the bridge across a river. They braked for the switch, and entered the siding, then, sanding the tracks, they came to an emergency stop.

As their pursuer shot past them at high speed, the two crewmembers were astonished to note that the train consisted only of a locomotive and its tender—no cars were being pulled. There appeared to be no one in the cab as the huge locomotive steamed by. What was going on?

It was then that the sidelined train was approached by a switchman. "Thank God you stopped!" he said. "How did you know that the bridge ahead just collapsed?" It seems that floating pack ice had jammed up against the bridge's supports, causing a key trestle to fail. If the local freight hadn't switched to a siding and stopped, it would have careened down into a narrow valley, probably killing the engineer and fireman. "We had to get out of the way of that special," said the engineer. "What special?" was the reply. No one else had seen or heard the phantom train that saved the local freight from disaster. Perhaps it was a very special train indeed.

Bibliography

Barry, William. *A Stroll Through the Past.* Portland, ME: Self-published, 1933.

Beck, Horace. *Folklore of Maine.* Philadelphia: J. B. Lippincott, 1957.

Botkin, B. A., (ed.). *A Treasury of American Folklore.* New York: Crown Publishers, 1944.

Clark, Jerome. *Unexplained!* Canton, MI: Visible Ink Press, 1999.

Coleman, Loren. *Mysterious America.* London: Faber and Faber, 1983.

Federal Writers' Project. *Maine: A Guide "Down East."* Boston: Houghton Mifflin, 1937.

Harper, Charles. *Haunted Houses: Tales of the Supernatural.* Philadelphia: J. B. Lippincott, 1930.

Hauck, Dennis. *Haunted Places: The National Directory.* New York: Penguin-Putnam, 2002.

Holzer, Hans. *Yankee Ghosts.* Indianapolis: Bobbs Merrill, 1963.

Jasper, Mark. *Haunted Inns of New England.* Yarmouth Port, MA: On Cape Publications, 2002.

Krantz, Les. *America by the Numbers: Facts and Figures from the Weighty to the Way-Out.* Boston: Houghlin Mifflin, 1993.

Myers, Arthur. *The Ghostly Register.* New York: McGraw-Hill/Contemporary Books, 1986.

Pickering, David. *Casell Dictionary of Superstitions.* London: Casell, 1995.

Pitkin, David. *Ghosts of the Northeast.* New York: Aurora Publications, 2002.

Robinson, Charles. *The New England Ghost Files.* North Attleboro, MA: Covered Bridge Press, 1994.

Schulte, Carol. *Ghosts on the Coast of Maine.* Sioux City, IA: Quixote Press, 1989.

Simpson, Dorothy. *The Maine Islands in Story and Legend.* Philadelphia: J. B. Lippincott, 1960.

Skinner, Charles. *American Myths and Legends*. Detroit: Gale Research Co., 1974.

———. *Myths and Legends of Our Own Land: As to Buried Treasure and Storied Waters, Cliffs and Mountains*. Philadelphia: J. B. Lippincott, 1896.

———. *Myths and Legends of Our Own Land: Tales of Puritan Land*. Philadelphia J. B. Lippincott, 1896.

Thomson, C. J. S. *The Mystery and Lore of Apparitions*. London: Harold Shaylor, 1930.

Verde, Thomas. *Maine Ghosts and Legends*. Camden, ME: Down East Books, 1989.

Verrill, Alpheus. *Romantic and Historic Maine*. New York: Dodd, Meade & Co., 1933.

Winthrop, John. *The History of New England From 1630–1649*. Edited by James Kendall. New York: Charles Scribner and Sons, 1908.

Acknowledgments

AT STACKPOLE BOOKS, EDITOR KYLE WEAVER PROVIDED THE EXPERT advice and friendly counsel so necessary to the completion of the manuscript, which was meticulously copyedited by Amy Wagner. Associate editor Amy Cooper skillfully guided the book through the production process. Heather Adel Wiggins drew the delightfully macabre illustrations. My old friend and onetime co-author, Patricia Martinelli, contributed many good suggestions. My good friend and colleague Laura Ruthig expertly word-processed the manuscript, once again demonstrating her uncanny ability to decipher my handwriting. I wish to thank those who graciously shared their encounters with the supernatural on the grounds of anonymity. They know how much I appreciate their help and their confidence. My lovely wife, Diane, patiently tolerated my preoccupation with yet another book and tried not to be irritated by untidy mounds of books and papers in our cozy nest.

About the Author

CHARLES A. STANSFIELD JR. HAS TAUGHT GEOGRAPHY AT ROWAN University for forty-one years and published fifteen textbooks on cultural and regional geography. In the course of his research, he realized that stories of ghosts and other strange phenomena reflect the history, culture, economy, and even physical geography of a region. He is the author of *Haunted Jersey Shore*, and co-author with Patricia A. Martinelli of *Haunted New Jersey*. This volume, the first of three focused on the northern New England States, grew out of his long-standing appreciation of the physical and cultural geography of the Pine Tree State.